STARTING SAILING

starting
sailing

James Moore and Alan Turvey

David & Charles NEWTON ABBOT

0 7153 6095 7

Illustrations by Alan Turvey

Film Set in Monophoto 9/11 Univers Medium by
Ramsay Typesetting Limited London
Printed in Great Britain by
Redwood Burn Limited Trowbridge and Esher
for David & Charles (Holdings) Limited
South Devon House   Newton Abbot   Devon

Contents

Introduction

We have produced *Starting Sailing* from the basic idea that a good graphic illustration speaks louder than words. Therefore the text has been kept to the absolute minimum, leaving the reader to spend most of his time studying the illustrations. Each drawing has a great deal to tell about the boat and its equipment, and about the sails and the way they are driving the craft. A drawing will illustrate several important points, and you should therefore take time to study each one very thoroughly, especially with regard to the crew's actions and activities. We do not pretend that we can teach sailing from illustration and text alone, but we think that anyone going afloat with a basic knowledge founded on *Starting Sailing* will certainly find things easier. The boat will appear more familiar, the manoeuvres much easier to comprehend.

We have chosen to illustrate all manoeuvres with the helmsman facing forward. It is a matter of opinion whether it is better to face aft or forward, and you will finally adopt the method you prefer. We think it is better to see where you are going all the time and learn one good sequence of movements.

Although we have chosen to illustrate the principles of sailing with a dinghy, the lessons learnt can equally well be applied to a small cruising boat.

A little philosophy

The sea, in fact any stretch of open water, is a place to be treated with respect. You should always be prepared to meet it in its worst moods. These moods are variable and change quickly. Fine weather can turn to foul in hours, even minutes. Always be sure that your boat is seaworthy, properly equipped and in tip-top condition. Remember, there are no convenient garages to call in if you should have a breakdown. Wear clothing appropriate to the weather, bearing in mind that when sailing you are exposed to the elements more than in most other sports. Check on local weather forecasts and do not go out if they predict really bad weather. Finally, sail within your limitations and that of the boat. Don't set off to cruise even short distances without being sure that you are equipped mentally, physically and materially to make the voyage successfully. Always carry a compass.

It may seem that a great deal of emphasis is placed on caution, thereby introducing a killjoy note. That is not our intention. What we want to emphasise is only that you cannot enjoy sailing properly unless you do it safely and have passed all the self-imposed tests of skill, which will then enable you to go afloat and be able to cope with all emergencies as they occur.

Joining a sailing club is a great way to enhance your possibilities of enjoyment from sailing. There you will meet people of common interest, you will be introduced to racing and be able to make friends with whom you can sail in company and with whom you can yarn about your experiences afterwards. Clubs, too, have immensely useful facilities like clubhouses, changing rooms, dinghy and car parks, launching ramps and rescue launches for those who race. All these things make sailing more pleasurable, so a good piece of advice is to get yourself along to a club at an early stage. You can either approach the secretary direct or get a friend or acquaintance who is a member to introduce you.

Earlier we said that we do not set out to teach sailing completely with this book; furthermore, we now say that one of the best things you can do before taking the risk of buying a boat without prior knowledge of what it is all about, is to attend a sailing school for a short course. This book will certainly help to make your course easier to understand and more worthwhile. A sailing course with good instructors will give you that essential confidence which may be a very long time coming if you go it alone right from the start. As with learning to drive a car, of course, the real problems come after the course is over and you are on your own, but at least you will have acquired basic knowledge and confidence.

Something we just cannot teach is the *feel* of your boat. That is something which only comes with practice, and to handle your boat really well and expertly in all conditions calls for fine judgement of its speed and handling qualities. Every boat is different, and you will easily get used to the characteristics of one you sail regularly. When you go out to practise in the early days, avoid moored boats, choosing instead an open stretch of water or a channel with little traffic. We recommend plenty of practice with tacking into the wind and gybing, as well as sailing close-hauled, which is the point of sailing which calls for most concentration.

There is insufficient room in this book to say much about what kind of boat to buy. Advice on this subject is best obtained by talking to experienced owners or explaining your needs to your sailing school instructor. If you join a yacht club you will probably want to buy one of the class boats adopted by the clubs. Yachting journals frequently feature types of boats and give advice to would-be owners. A few basic rules apply. Buy within your capabilities, i.e. as a beginner don't be tempted to a high-powered racing machine; buy a really seaworthy type of boat, fully equipped; if you are keen on a small cruiser, put sailing performance before all other considerations – no boat will be much good if it will not perform well under sail; be sure that you can handle the boat in and out of the water easily unless it is the type which lies permanently on a mooring.

Taking care of your boat
This is not intended as a comprehensive account of everything you should do before and after you sail, but a basic guide to keeping the craft in shipshape order.

At all times keep the hull clean and well-painted. Always repair minor damage immediately. Keep dirt and sand out of the inside where it might clog bailers and get into blocks and other moving parts. Take a pride in keeping your boat looking like new inside and out (it will enhance its second-hand value anyway). More than in any other sphere of activity, people who exhibit such seamanlike tendencies invariably prove to be thoughtful and good sailors.

Before going afloat make the following checks:

1. All standing rigging sound and properly attached to mast and hull.
2. All running rigging correctly rigged and running free.
3. All fittings attached firmly to mast and hull, showing no signs of coming loose.
4. Buoyancy sound, properly fastened.
5. All opening hatches secured – put the bungs in!

After coming ashore, wash the boat down with fresh water and remove loose gear to safe storage. Wash sails from time to time, especially if you sail in salt water, and examine frequently for damage. Inspect all ropes for signs of chafe and rigging for signs of damage or excessive wear. If your boat is one you leave on the mooring, stow all the gear neatly away in its correct places, ropes 7 coiled, loose gear like sail battens, tiller, etc., lashed firmly in place. Store neatly in lockers in the club for complete safety. Always remember that failure of the boat or gear is likely to happen when it is least easy to deal with (i.e. in bad weather), and that you will probably have only your own resources to call upon to get you out of immediate trouble. It makes sense to do everything to avoid such occurrences. A good idea is to carry a bosun's bag of tools and bits and pieces for use in an emergency. You need pliers, a good knife with a marlinespike, whipping twine, sailmakers' needles and palm, copper wire, spare shackles and split pins. In fact, you can make up your own list according to the gear your boat carries.

Other snags

Get to know a sailing area before venturing out. Local knowledge can be invaluable, especially about tides, sand banks, hidden rocks and the like. If you sail in tidal waters be sure you get an up-to-date tide table. A proper sea chart is not expensive, but is a complete mine of information. You can buy either a special yachtsmans' chart if one exists or otherwise an official mariners' chart. Reading a chart is not difficult, but you should ask someone knowledgeable to explain the special signs or get a book which will do this for you.

Launch only in places specially appointed for this purpose or in places where you are quite certain it is safe to do so, like a gently shelving beach with no breakers and little current. If in doubt ask, or watch, where other experienced people do it.

If you want to race

Competition is one of the finest aspects of sailing. You will probably be drawn to it, but don't attempt it until you can handle your boat really competently, almost by instinct. Your reactions need to be that much faster if you race. You need, too, to know the yacht racing rules properly. Buy *Paul Elvstrom Explains* – it's easily the best small book you can have on the subject of the rules.

You can only race if you join a recognised club and we have already mentioned the advantages of this in a general way.

PART 1

Getting ready to sail

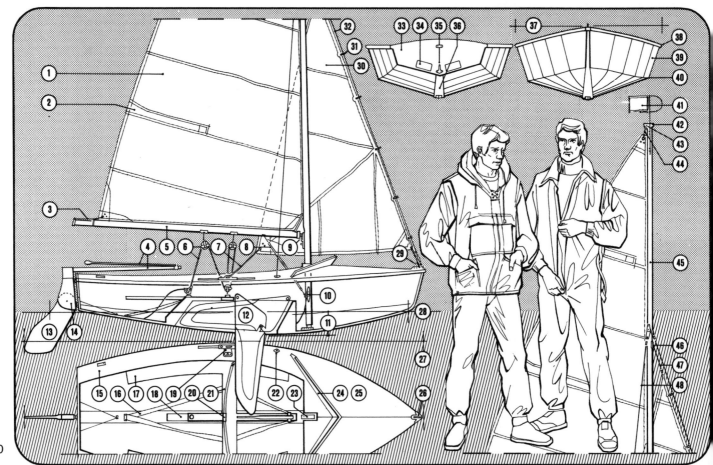

The first things with which you must acquaint yourself are the parts of the boat. Here we show all the essential pieces of a sailing dinghy. Later on we explain more about the sails [see page 33]. Whilst dinghies differ in detail and size they all work in the same way and so do small cruisers. You won't have any difficulty in adapting your knowledge to

Parts of the boat

1. Mainsail (usually terylene dacron but can be cotton)
2. Batten (pocket)
3. Clew line
4. Tiller with extension
5. Boom (spruce or alloy)
6. Mainsheet with tackle
7. Foresheet
8. Kicking strap
9. Gooseneck
10. Halyard cleat
11. Waterline
12. Centreboard (plate)
13. Rudder blade
14. Rudder stock
15. Side-deck
16. Toe straps
17. Side thwart
18. Centreboard case
19. Foresheet leads or fairleads
20. Mainsheet track
21. Main thwart
22. Shroud plate
23. Mast step
24. Breakwater
25. Foredeck
26. Stemhead fitting
27. Overall length
28. Waterline length
29. Rigging screw (stainless steel)
30. Foresail (material as for mainsail)
31. Foresail hauls
32. Forestay (galvanised or stainless steel wire)
33. Transom
34. Transom flags
35. Rudder gudgeon and pintle
36. Keel
37. Beam
38. Gunwale
39. Topsides
40. Chine
41. Racing flag
42. Masthead
43. Main halyard sleeve
44. Main halyard
45. Mast (spruce or alloy)
46. Fore halyard sleeve
47. Fore halyard (galvanised or stainless steel wire)
48. Main shroud

It is very important that you learn all the parts of the boat by heart so that you will not be at a loss if you are asked by someone to do something or get hold of a particular piece. Get a friend to test your knowledge with a real boat. 11

Here you can see the essential difference between the dinghy and the small cruiser. In the former the basic stability is provided by the crew, their number depending on the size and type of boat. As the boat heels they move their weight out to counteract the thrust of the wind, or spill excessive wind from the sails by easing the sheets a little, or yet again, head the boat into the wind to relieve the pressure; failure to do any of these could lead to a capsize. Sitting out or hiking, as it is called, can be assisted by either a trapeze (a wire attached to the mast, on which the crew is suspended) or by a sliding seat (very uncommon these days). Some stability is provided by the weight of the boat and by its beam – the beamier the boat, the stiffer it is (a stiff boat heels little). The resistance of the centreboard and the rudder also help.

The dinghy crew have therefore to be very agile people, but a prerequisite of the dinghy is sufficient buoyancy to support not only itself and its gear; but the crew as well, once a capsize has occurred.

The cruiser relies much more, indeed almost entirely in many cases, on the heavy ballast keel (or keels, if the boat is a twin-bilge keel cruiser). The crew can even sit down to leeward without fear of capsize. Such boats may possibly be laid flat in heavy winds but the pendulum effect of the keel will right the craft if the crew spill wind or head to windward. Because of her design she ships very little water.

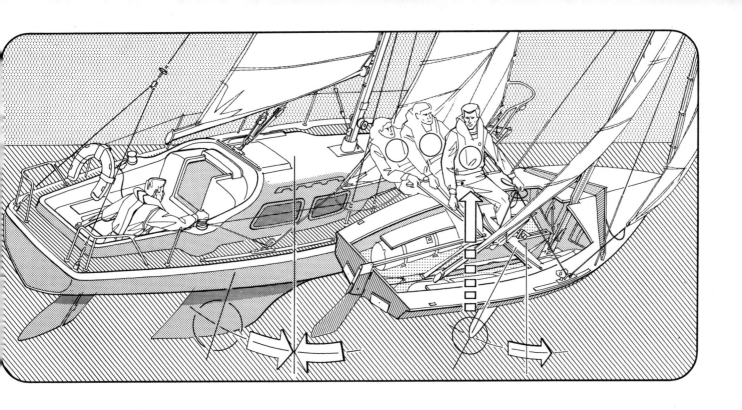

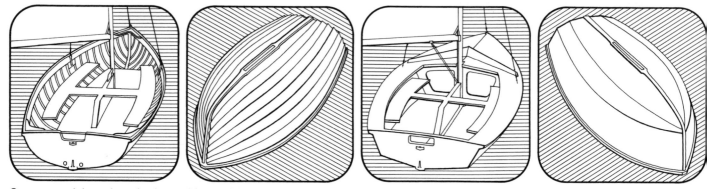

Some materials and methods used in small boat construction.

Top, left to right. Carvel, smooth wood planks edge on; expensive. Clinker, wood planks overlapping; expensive. Single chine – using marine-grade ply; easy for home construction. Double chine – also ply.
Bottom, left to right. Combined clinker and chine, using marine ply. Cold- or hot-moulded laminated wood veneers over a plug; expensive. GRP; fibre glass laminate and resin from a mould. EPS; expanded polystyrene, also made by mould principle.

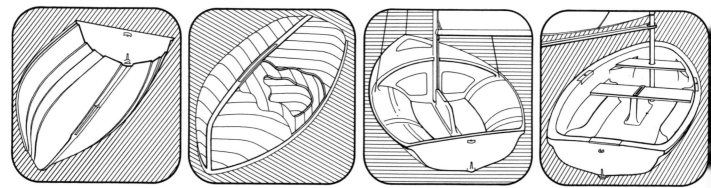

Essential basic parts of the hull and centreboard.

A   Centreboard case.
B   Main thwart.
C   Hog (internal part of keel).
D   Centreboard bolt.
     Arrows indicate slot for centreboard.
W   Waterline.

A   Direction of insertion.
B   Main thwart and board stop.
C   Jamb block (usually rubber) to keep board in any chosen position.
D   Bolt on which board pivots. A sleeve will prevent wear.
E   Stops to prevent board going right through case and give handholds.
F   Profile of board.
G   Slot in bottom of boat closed by rubber strips when board is up.
H   Large washers (inner one waterproof) to prevent damage to board case.
     Note: form of bolt illustrated prevents case being pinched and strained as bolt is tightened.

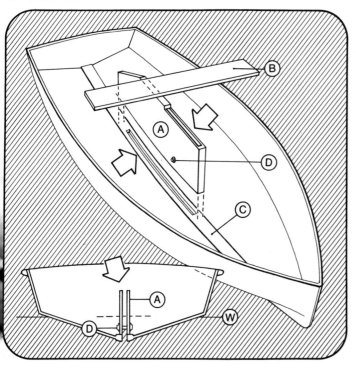

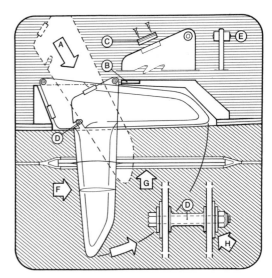

15

Here are four rigs most commonly seen on sailing craft today.

The *Optimist*, which is an ideal children's boat, is most unusual in having a *spritsail rig*, but this is very convenient for stowing the spars in the boat for transport. You must not expect high efficiency from the sails when sailing to windward.

The *Mirror* dinghy is also an ideal beginner's boat for both children and adults, but has a more efficient rig called a *gunter rig*. Here again the spars will stow inside the boat for transportation.

The most efficient rig of all is the *bermudan rig*, where the luff of the mainsail is one continuous straight line from top to bottom. We illustrate a *420* which is a typical two-man fast dinghy, widely sailed throughout the world. The *bermudan rig* can also be used as a single sail rig (sometimes known as *cat rigged*). Note the mast is further forward than on the *420*. The *OK* is a fast racing craft for single-handed sailing.

When choosing your first boat be very careful to buy something uncomplicated and within your capabilities. Also, be sure to buy something big enough to carry all the people you may want to carry. It is easy to be swayed by considerations like ease of handling ashore or on a roof rack, but these would be of secondary importance. If you buy a class of boat popular in your area you can always sell it again more easily when you want to graduate to something better.

Buoyancy is essential in any boat which can capsize. It should be high at the gunwales, above the centre of gravity, and evenly distributed fore and aft, floating the boat so the crew can get on the centreboard as illustrated. It must support the boat, gear and crew indefinitely when all are completely waterlogged.

Well-positioned buoyancy will help right the boat once the crew has exerted initial leverage. Unless your boat is designed to be completely self-bailing, a large bailer or soft plastic bucket should be carried, attached to the boat with a length of line.

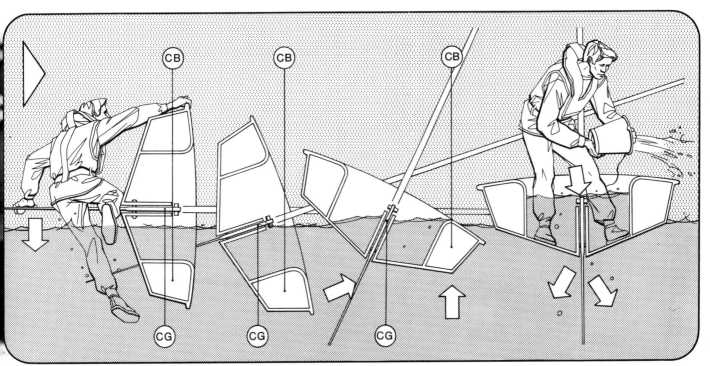

The function of a properly designed *life-jacket* is to ensure that the wearer will float face up. It is essential to buy one to support your own particular weight. Some expensive ones will inflate automatically when the wearer enters the water – the majority are inflated by mouth. Others have a measure of built-in buoyancy, but tend to be bulky.

Buoyancy aids (bottom row) distribute the bulk round the figure, permitting great ease of movement, which is useful in a small dinghy, especially when climbing aboard after a capsize, but some will not necessarily support an unconscious person or turn him on his back. All beginners and inexperienced sailors should wear a *life-jacket*, whatever the weather.

It would be difficult to make it a legal requirement for every sailor to be able to swim, but we think that every sailor should be able to do so and to be able to make his way through the water for some 25 metres (82 feet) fully clothed, wearing light trousers and shirt plus sailing shoes which can, of course, be kicked off. This latter manoeuvre you can practice in the local swimming pool. How far you should be able to swim is less important than an ability to stay afloat without assistance almost indefinitely. If you want to set yourself a swimming target then we suggest 200 metres (650 feet) of any stroke you like, backstroke included.

The ability to swim is an insurance against the day when a capsize occurs and you or your crew have no life-jacket on, and against the day when a life-jacket may fail. In any event, it is most unwise to rely solely on the life-jacket with its built-in support and be quite unable to move through the water to the boat or some other object.

This emphasis on swimming is to a large extent prompted by a recognition of the need for people who sail to have a strong in-built sense of self-preservation. Nothing saps your confidence faster if you are thrown suddenly into the water than to discover that you just don't know how to stay afloat, let alone get anywhere. Being able to swim moderately well and stay afloat for some time, we suggest, will remove one fear from your mind and make sailing more enjoyable. In any case, it's hardly fair on your skipper to make him responsible for looking after you as well as the boat. In the days when we regularly sailed dinghies we were pretty tough about taking non-swimmers, and it is a rule which we would not want to waive. Even in a small cruising yacht the danger of someone falling overboard is not entirely remote. Make sure you and your crew can swim and stay afloat, even though life-jackets may always be worn.

Safety does not consist only in wearing a life-jacket or being able to swim. Throughout this book we will be pointing out things like weather, good equipment, knowledge of the tides and so on, all of which have a bearing on safety. It is sufficient here to emphasise the necessity for making safety a prime aspect of going afloat. After all, if sailing should get a reputation for being unsafe you can be sure that legislation would soon make an appearance as it has on the roads and this would be most undesirable in a sport.

Of course, you don't need to dress up in regulation gear to sail, but there is a good deal of practical and attractive specialised clothing on the market today. The main thing is to keep warm and dry. The biggest risk is from exposure, which can occur all too easily on the water. In cooler climates and on cold days, full length suits are a godsend In warmer weather and for ease of movement you can stick to shorts.

The two people, extreme right, are wearing wet suits which add immeasurably to warmth as well as contributing a small amount of extra buoyancy. Highly recommended for cold weather and rough conditions.

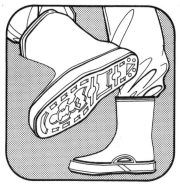

Good footwear is essential. Profiled soles give you positive grip on wet slippery surfaces. Neoprene socks protected by cheap plastic sandals, or neoprene bootees, keep feet warm. The sandals alone allow the feet to dry quickly in warm weather. Short boots, apt to fill with water, are suitable for cruisers.

Tight cuffs stop water running up your sleeves. Make sure your watch is waterproof. Ski bands and pigtails keep long hair out of eyes. Gloves protect sensitive hands from chafe from ropes. A towel around the neck keeps cold spray from running down to your vitals. A peak cap shades the eyes and keeps unruly hair in place.

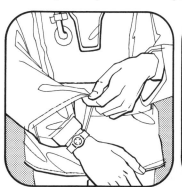

The weather

In no other sport is the weather of such vital importance. There are all too few balmy days when sailing is an unalloyed pleasure of idly slipping through the water, the ripples playfully slapping the bows and lapping their way along the waterline. It therefore pays to know what is likely to happen before going afloat. Radio forecasts, especially wind forecasts, are useful but often very general. Local area forecasts can be obtained through special shipping forecasts or sometimes by a telephone weather service. Airports and coastguard services will also supply reliable weather information. Acquaint yourself with the Beaufort scale of wind speeds [see opposite page], so that you are at least aware of the results of certain wind speeds on the sea and can judge if the weather is likely to make conditions too rough for you.

With a little knowledge anyone can become, to some extent, a forecaster of immediate events. Recognition of what kind of clouds are in the sky combined with wind directions will enable you to determine whether the conditions will improve or deteriorate. The most useful book published on this subject is *Instant Weather Forecasting* by Alan Watts. We recommend you to buy it. Always keep half an eye on the weather. Watch for thunderstorms, rain squalls, sudden shifts of wind and imminent calms. Although bad weather usually means strong winds, never forget that one of the worst possible conditions is no wind combined with thick sea fog. Carry a small compass for such an eventuality.

Local areas

All sailing areas have their local peculiarities. Discuss them with someone with local knowledge and get them to show you on a chart places to avoid. Find out the dangerous winds and their directions (particularly important if there are high cliffs and mountains nearby). Ask too about currents and tides, especially rips which can cause a nasty sea with the wind in a certain direction.

In the early stages do not go out when no other craft are at sea. In any event stay around near boats which are obviously not bound for other areas. Tell your friends and relatives that you are going afloat and how long you think you will be.

There are no absolutely safe places to sail, but some are better than others. Choose sheltered estuaries with little current for your first excursions. For obvious reasons you should always stay within sight of land.

Cardinal rules for beginners

In hot, sunny weather it is not uncommon to find early in the day that the weather is calm and winds variable, sometimes from all points of the compass. As the land heats up a sea breeze comes in. This rarely exceeds force 2–3 and makes a fine sailing wind. At evening, as the land cools, the process is reversed and winds blow off the land, usually at the same strength. Take these into account if you are sailing late in the day in such fine weather.

Don't sail far offshore with an offshore wind.

Don't sail offshore at all with an offshore wind and ebb tide.

Don't go sailing, until you are experienced, where there are no lookout or rescue facilities or frequent harbours or anchorages. Sailing near a yacht club is a pretty safe bet.

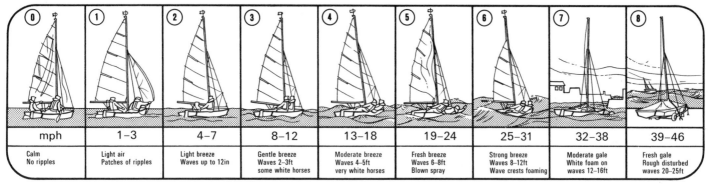

0	1	2	3	4	5	6	7	8
mph	1–3	4–7	8–12	13–18	19–24	25–31	32–38	39–46
Calm No ripples	Light air Patches of ripples	Light breeze Waves up to 12in	Gentle breeze Waves 2–3ft some white horses	Moderate breeze Waves 4–5ft very white horses	Fresh breeze Waves 6–8ft Blown spray	Strong breeze Waves 8–12ft Wave crests foaming	Moderate gale White foam on waves 12–16ft	Fresh gale Rough disturbed waves 20–25ft

The Beaufort wind scale

Four typical cloud formations. Left to right.

Fair weather cumulus. This denotes settled conditions at least temporarily. No strong winds.

Low cloud associated with strong winds up to gale force. Fierce squalls in gaps.

Thunder cloud. Watch for speed of build-up and head for home.

If it moves fast towards you it will come against the surface wind and bring abrupt changes of wind direction with *very* strong squalls and probably rain. Dowse all sail and anchor. If you cannot anchor, put out a sea anchor and keep head to wind.

Approaching front. Will bring rain and often more wind.

23

When you first arrive at your destination have a good look round. Note exactly where people are launching, what the wind direction and strength is and which way the current is flowing (if any). If the area is tidal, find out immediately the state of the tides. Tides occur twice every twenty-four hours, except in certain unusual locations such as the Solent, England. Tides will run fiercest in narrow channels, and spring tides (very high ones) will flood and ebb faster than neap tides (very low tides). If possible, study a tidal chart of the area to get an idea of the particular currents.

We have mentioned already the snags to look for and the knowledge needed. Here the two figures are checking on the suitability of the sailing area, before rushing off. Note they are both in possession of life-jackets. Study the boat and its gear and the general neat and tidy way things are prepared. They will probably chat to the couple going down the slipway to get further useful advice. The boat sailing in the middle of the channel will give them a very good indication of the wind strength.

Some road trailers can be used for launching, but they *must* be the type that have sealed bearings. Moreover, they must be adequately painted against rust. It is better to transfer the boat to a launching trolley, which is lighter, simpler and has bearings which can be easily greased or, being solid, will stand water immersion better. First the bow is lifted to insert the trolley. Then the whole boat is moved across using the bow chock as the fulcrum. Even light dinghies are better handled by *two people*. A rupture is easily caused by trying to lift too much weight on your own. It is important to keep feet close together and lift in unison, carrying the boat over smoothly. Launching trolley has padded chocks for protection of boat bottom.

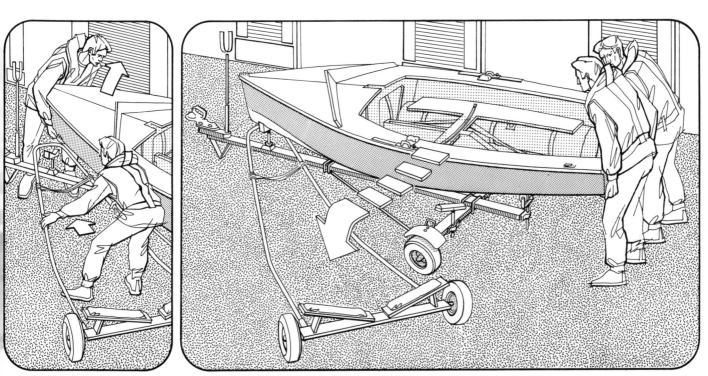

Make bow fast to the arm of trolley, so that boat cannot slip back when moved. Check buoyancy bags and inflate if necessary. Wipe boat down to keep sails clean and lay boat on cover to protect bottom. To insert or remove a launching trolley from under boat, see third illustration below. One man can do this if he is strong enough and does not attempt to lift the boat too high. The secret is to ease the trolley under the boat a little at a time. Same applies when removing trolley. This must be done slowly or there is a danger of the boat dropping suddenly with resultant damage. It is essential to have a launching trolley which is big enough for the boat. Try to choose one which is light as well.

When trailing long distances leave centreboard out of boat if it is wood and insert before launching. To do this spread the boat cover or other protective material on the ground (choosing an area without stones or gravel if possible) and list her over on her side. This may need two people, but the boat can be held in position by one as shown, while the second man inserts the centreboard.

The next stage is to check the rigging on the mast, sort it all out making sure it is not kinked and get ready to step the mast. Tie all the loose ends of rigging at the lower end of the mast with a lanyard.

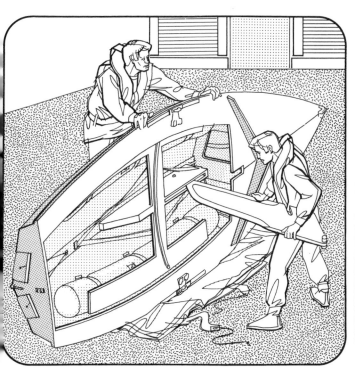

Stepping the mast

The main and fore halyards are made fast to the mast. Spinnaker or whisker pole fittings are the ideal place. Check that both halyards and burgee halyard run freely in the sheeves. Make fast halyard to cleats at base of mast. Stay shackles can be taped or wired to prevent them coming loose. Split pins should be taped to prevent possible sail damage. The first stage in stepping the mast is to attach the main shrouds, in this case, to a common type of adjustable shroud plate, situated under the deck for neatness and to reduce windage. Whilst this is being done the crew can take the weight off the upper part of the mast.

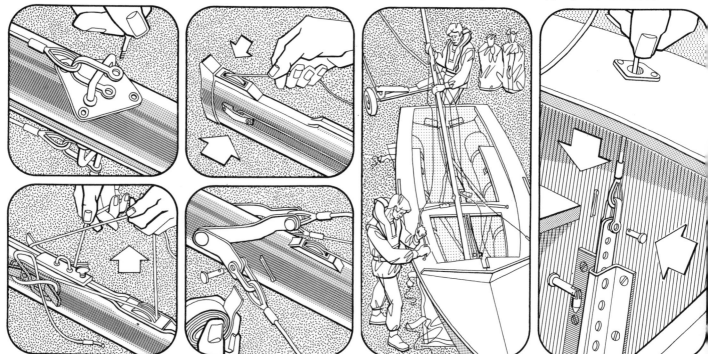

To step the mast, one man stands in the dinghy (be sure that it is well-chocked and supported underneath). The other man holds the forestay and helps by pulling gently and steadying the mast as the other locates the foot in the step.

Mast steps are often adjustable in several directions. This enables you to position the mast in the best place for the boat's performance. You will have to experiment to find this.

The forestay is attached by a rigging screw. Use a rod or screwdriver shank to adjust the tension, tighten lock nuts and make fast with wire as indicated so that it cannot unscrew.

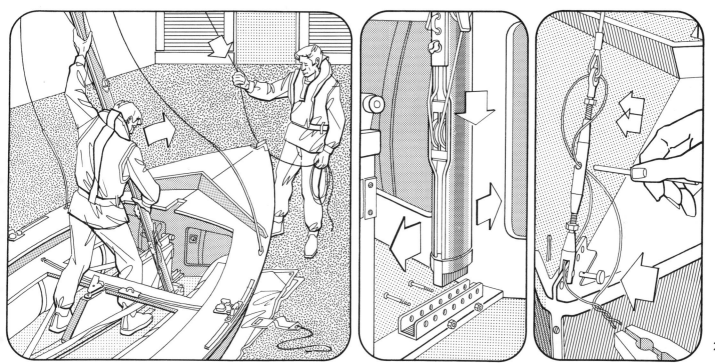

To adjust mast rake, first ensure that the boat is quite level (use a spirit level). Note the crew placing this on the main thwart to test that the boat is level in both directions. Attach a weight to the main halyard (buy a lead weight, or use a piece of 100 grammes [4 ounces] metal). The mast must be vertical in a lateral direction and this is adjusted with the shrouds. The fore and aft angle, called rake, is adjusted on the forestay. The most desirable rake is something you will have to ascertain for yourself and will depend on the boat, its class, and its sails. On the following page we explain the effects of rake, so that you can see why you must get it right.

The perfectly balanced boat 'pivots' round an imaginary centre point, indicated by the dotted line. If the mast is raked too far forward then the pressures exerted forward to this line will tend to push the bow away. This is *lee helm*. The helmsman counteracts by pushing the tiller away. *Lee helm* is dangerous. If the mast is raked too far aft then the boat tends to come up into the wind. This is *weather helm*. The helmsman counteracts by pulling the tiller towards him. Should he have to do this too much the boat goes slower as the rudder drags a lot. The ideal situation is where there is just a *little* weather helm, so that the boat would come gently into the wind by itself if the helm was left.

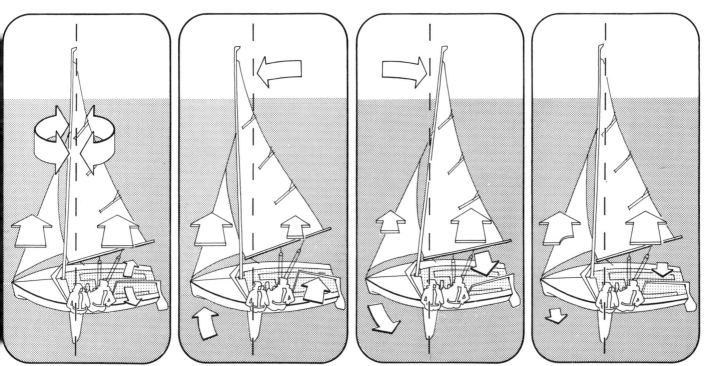

A burgee or racing flag is not simply to identify your club or show you are racing. It is an important indicator, giving wind direction and to some extent strength. The way the after end of the flag flaps will show whether the wind is light or fresh. Using the halyard, attach the burgee stick with clove hitches, ensuring the lower one is near the bottom of the stick. Pull both tight. Ensure your flag rotates freely on the stick and see that, when hoisted, it stands up straight (the halyard must be taut). To clear all rigging when you hoist, dip the top as illustrated allowing the wind to take the flag away from the mast until it is up. Before hoisting sails, turn the boat into wind.

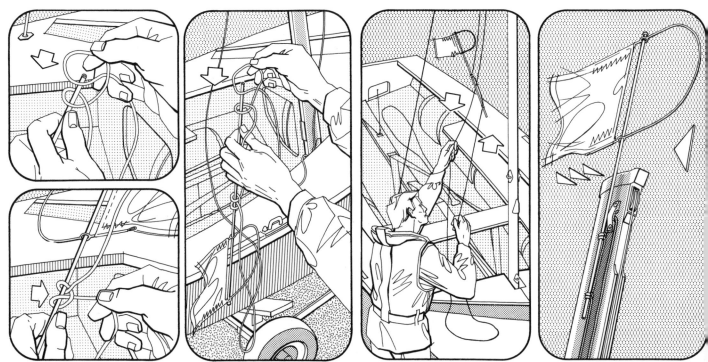

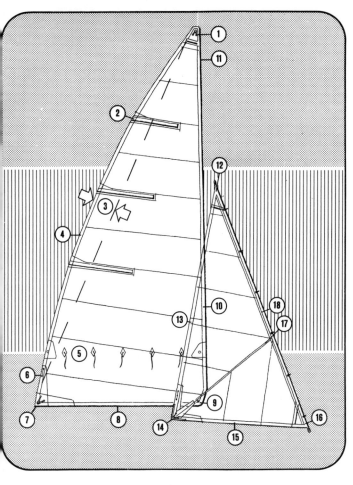

Parts of the sail – mainsail and foresail, also called commonly jib.

Main

1. Headboard
2. Batten pocket
3. Roach (extent indicated by dotted line)
4. Leech
5. Reef points
6. Leech line (uncommon on terylene [dacron] sails)
7. Clew
8. Foot
9. Tack
10. Luff
11. Luff rope (on small boats often used in conjunction with groove in mast for hoisting) otherwise clips and track are used (see separate diagrams on next page)

Jib

12. Head
13. Luff
14. Clew
15. Foot
16. Tack
17. Mitre seam
18. Jib Luff (usually with wire inside)

Your sails are your motive power, the equivalent of your engine in a car, and since they will be called upon time and again to sail you and your crew out of possible dangers (i.e. off a lee shore, to get you home against a foul wind and tide and to hurry you along on a wet, cold day), they cannot be looked after too carefully.

Although they do not stretch like cotton sails, to some extent even modern terylene (dacron) sails can be distorted when new. They should be treated with great care until they have settled down. When the sails are brand new, sail only in light weather, thus avoiding excessive sheeting-in or hard tensions on the luff and foot as needed in strong winds. When you set the mainsail for the first time, aim for an even, light tension along the boom. The main halyard tension effects the position of the draft of the sail (the highest point of camber when the sail forms its aerodynamic shape). In light winds the draft should fall slightly nearer the mast than halfway along the boom.

Once the sails have been 'run in' and you wish to sail in stronger winds, a little more tension on the halyard will move the draft further forward. Avoid overstretching the foot which is not so critical to the set of the sail.

The jib halyard must be set up tight for *all* wind conditions (a wire luff facilitates this). The tension on the jib foot and leach is controlled by the sheet and the correct positioning of the fairleads *[see page 41]*.

All sail parts are subject to chafe, and you should periodically go over the whole sail. Get small repairs done at once by your sailmaker. Washing periodically in mild detergent will keep sails clean and supple.

Below left to right:
Main halyard attached to headboard. Bolt-rope reinforced where it enters mast grove.
Some wooden masts have track and slides.
The sail battens keep the roach standing and prevent curl on the leech.
Leech line, not all that common now, can also correct leech curl and flap.

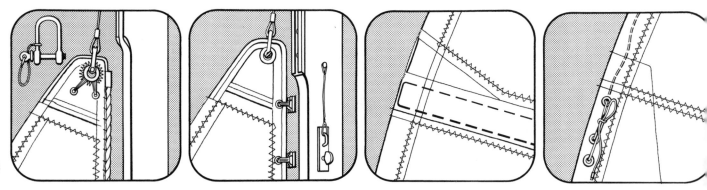

34

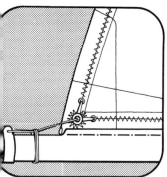

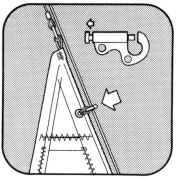

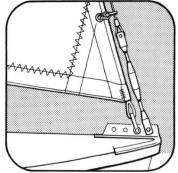

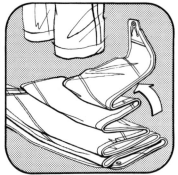

Method of lacing clew to boom called *outhaul*. Tail of lacing can also be taken through eyelet and around boom. Below, common method of fastening tack.

Piston hanks are used for attaching jib to forestay. Nylon or ss clips are also used. On some boats the jib is set flying, but sail performance is affected. Below, the clew of the jib.

Attach jib tack to stemhead fitting independently with its own shackle. Roll jibs up to stow so that luff wires do not kink.

Fold mainsail keeping luff sections parallel to maintain good shape. Then stow sails in bags clearly marked. The ones shown have ideal carrying handles.

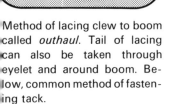

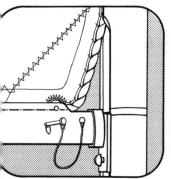

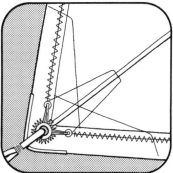

Setting the jib with the boat head to wind. First lay the jib on the fore deck, remember it was wiped clean for this purpose. Identify the parts, ensure it is not twisted. Shackle the tack down first.

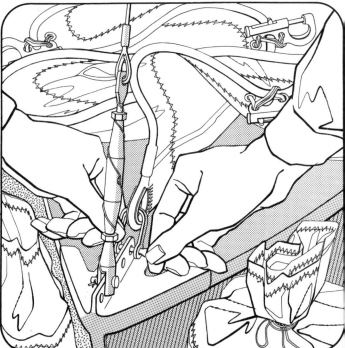

Piston hanks are common on larger dinghies. These are opened by pulling spring back and clipping over stay. Work from the tack up to the head.

Release jib halyard from mast and ensure it is clear of all other rigging and will not foul when hoisted.

Ease off enough halyard so that you can attach it to head of jib.

Be sure to make figure-of-eight knot in end of halyard or it may disappear up the mast!

37

There are various methods of attaching the foresheets, including using a shackle. The method shown is the neatest, and there is nothing to snag on the mast or in the rigging. You can leave the sheets permanently attached to the jib or undo the simple seizing each time. Since sheets need washing from time to time in fresh water, keep the method of attachment simple. We don't like shackles – they can damage the mast or the crew as they flail about in the breeze.

Take end of sheets *outside* the shrouds and through the fairleads.

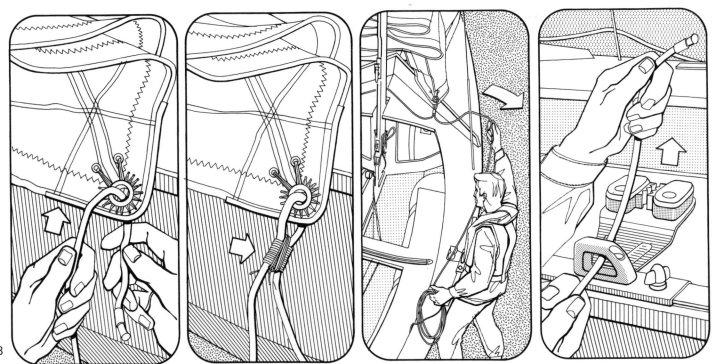

Immediately tie a figure-of-eight knot in the end of rope to prevent it slipping back through fairlead (a figure-of-eight is easy to undo and makes a sizeable knot). *Never* use a simple half-hitch or granny knot.

Here we show typical jamb cleats with serrated jaws.

Jamb cleats enable members of a boat's crew to operate the jib without perpetually having to strain to hold the sheet against wind pressure. When the rope is pulled through to take up slack, the jamb cleats open and grip the rope when pressure is released. To ease the sheet, jerk upwards and it comes free.

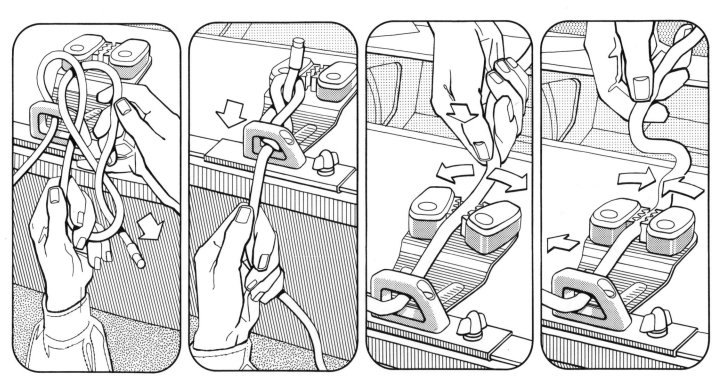

The best angle between the centreline of the boat and the fairleads varies with wind strength and the size of the jib from 9 degrees to 15 degrees. Some boats have a single fixed position, but many have adjustable fairleads with which you can experiment for best performance.

Haul the jib up very tight. The method shown here of sweating in the jib halyard is easy and will give good tension on most small boats. How tight? A good guide is to have the jib luff slightly tighter than the forestay.

The halyard should be pre-stretched synthetic rope or a combination of wire and pre-stretched synthetic rope for the best results. The luff will then stay taut.

Another method of jib-luff tensioning is for one man to pull the forestay out while the other tightens the halyard. Some boats have tensioners for internal halyards, which are easily adjustable for different sails and wind conditions. A tight jib luff is *essential* for good performance close to the wind. Many dinghies have jib fairleads adjustable fore and aft. The crew can adjust the tension on the foot and luff of the sail. Pulling the fairlead aft puts more tension on the foot of the sail, moving it forward produces more tension on the leech. If fairleads are not adjustable, the height of the tack can be varied by using a strop giving the same effect. A tight foot means the sail will be fuller near the top.

A tight leech means the sail will be fuller near the bottom. Adjust to get an even fullness all the way up. Make a point of marking the setting, so you can quickly adjust your fairlead again to this position to maintain the best setting for this particular sail.

Once it is set you want the jib out of the way until you have got afloat. Some very good jib rollers are now made. They can be used for reefing the jib as well as furling it.

If your boat is simple or you don't want to spend unnecessary money, roll the sail up and make fast with cotton ties which break easily when the sheet is pulled, or simply tuck it in between the luff and forestay as illustrated. If winds are very light you may not have to bother.

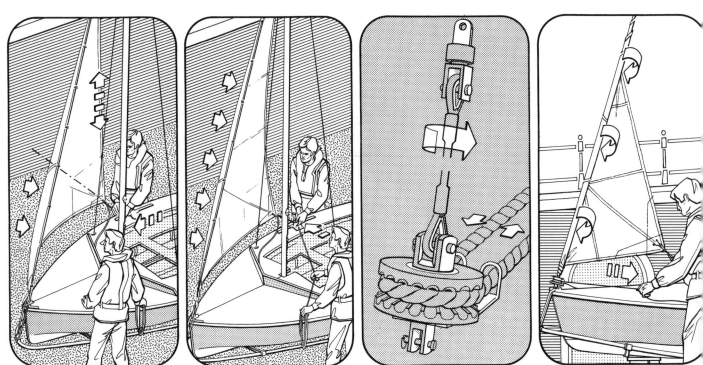

We have shown jib adjustment taking place on land, but the same procedures hold good if you do them afloat. Adjustments in sail setting are best experimented with ashore or, if afloat, in pretty calm weather.

Now rig the main.

Make sure the foot and luff are untwisted. If you fold as we have suggested they will never be twisted. If you don't fold, a good tip is to stow head-first into the bag, pulling out foot-first.

Slide in foot from mast end of boom, pulling gently and make sure there are no folds or creases caught up.

A little candle wax on the groove will minimise any possible chafe. Be sure groove opening has no sharp edges or snags.

One man feeds the sail in as the other pulls it along. Fasten tack (mast end) before fastening clew.

You should check frequently that the lacing is in good order and is properly fastened to the sail.

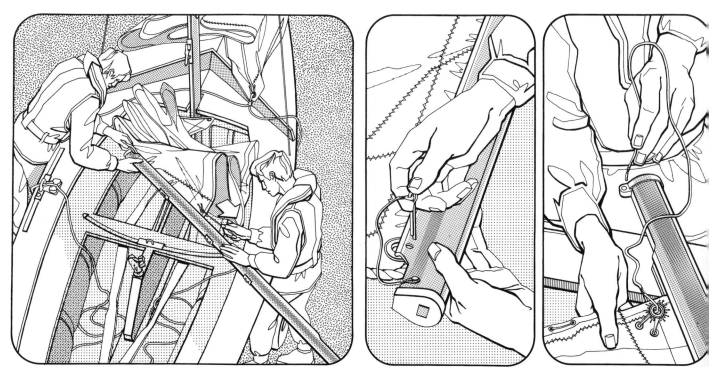

Make the clew fast, making sure that the lanyard is also wound round the boom, preferably passing through the clew eye. Sail tension along the boom will depend on the weather. Fairly tight for fresh winds, less tension for light airs [see page 48].

Push in the sail battens, thin end first if they are tapered. Number them to make sure you put them in the right pockets.

Battens must be smooth and should be of such a length that you have to push against the elastic end of the pocket. If your sail does not have this kind of pocket then tie in with a reef knot [see page 109]. In any event, the batten should not project beyond the edge of the sail.

Battens must always be somewhat flexible, never stiff, or the

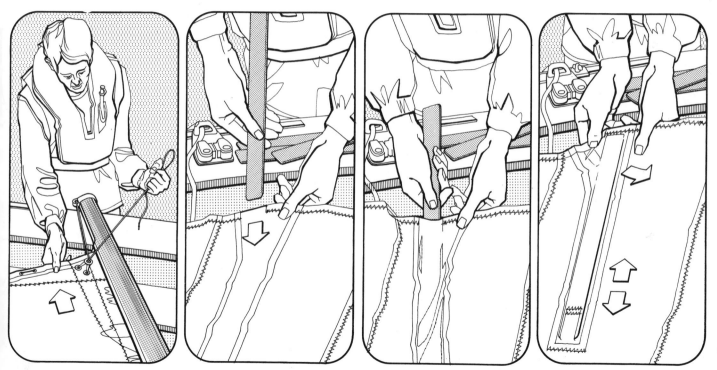

sail cannot take on a curve.

Next attach the mainsheet to the boom, making sure there is plenty of slack at this stage.

Then attach the main halyard and hoist the sail, one man feeding the luff (bolt rope or slides) into the track, the other hauling on the halyard. Be careful that you do not pull the halyard through its bottom block too obliquely or it will chafe badly.

One man feeds the sail in while the other pulls, until the point is reached when the weight of the boom is going to come on the sail. One man then takes the weight of the boom until the sail is

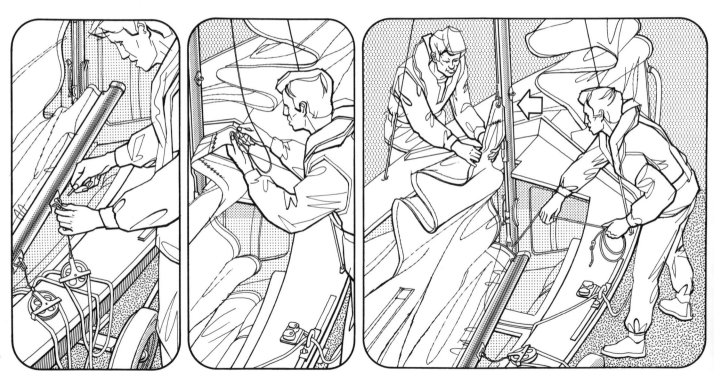

fully hoisted. At this stage the boom is attached to the gooseneck fitting. These vary a lot and we have illustrated a simple square spike which can be inserted in a square hole in the end of the boom.

This type enables you to ease the boom back to reef the sail by rolling it round the boom *[see next page]*. The boom can be attached to the gooseneck before the sail is hoisted, in which case it is quite essential for one man to lift the outboard end of the boom before any strain is placed on the leech of the sail. Each member of the crew must be able to raise or lower the main on their own.

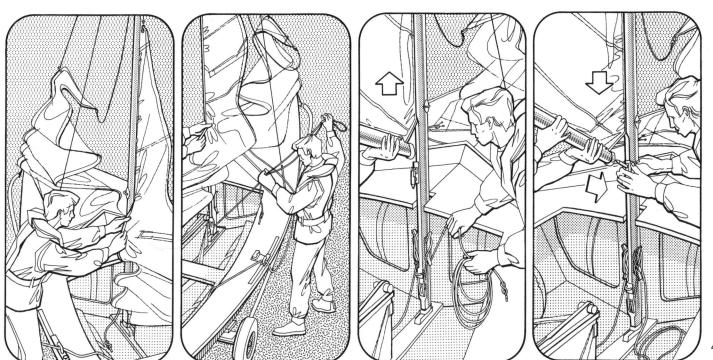

Here is the mainsail hoisted and the foot and luff tensions being adjusted. We have explained how this is done on the foot. The luff is usually tensioned by a sliding gooseneck fitting such as we show. Failing this the main halyard must be sweated up as we described for the jib. The other small diagram shows just how the sail can be rolled round the boom with this type of fitting, thus reefing the sail for strong winds.

A recap of mainsail tension – tight foot and tight luff give a flat sail, ideal for strong winds, slack foot and slack luff give a full sail, ideal for light airs.

Next, fit the kicking strap.

The kicking strap's purpose is simply to prevent the boom from

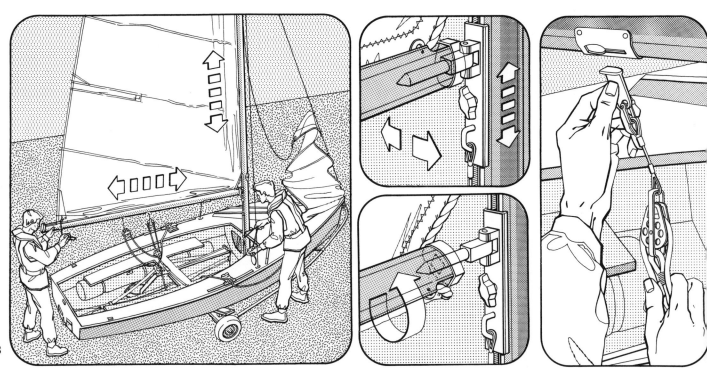

lifting in strong winds, thus allowing the sail's leech to go slack resulting in loss of aerofoil shape. It is especially valuable on the run when it controls the sail area particularly well and eliminates the danger of a Chinese gybe [see page 79].

Here we see the loss of shape and consequent loss of useful wind from the sail, with the boom right off, which is rapidly corrected by pulling the strap in hard. On the right we see the effects on the actual shape of the sail with the mainsheet rather harder in. The sail actually takes a reverse twist at the top and a huge curve on the leech. As soon as the kicking strap is taken in, the leech is faired up and the sail takes on a very even shape, which gives maximum performance, especially to windward.

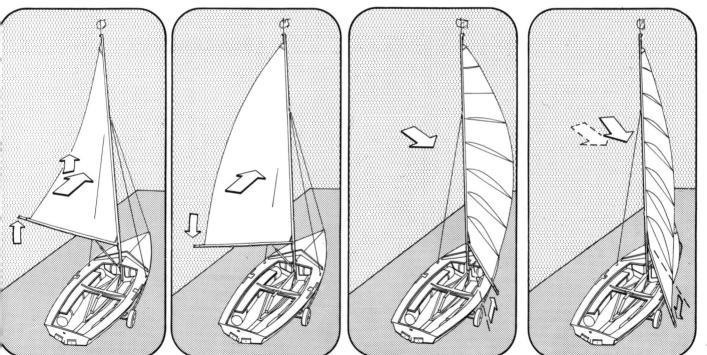

A mainsheet attached centrally to the boom is now regarded as giving most effective control over sail shape. The mainsheet shown is attached to a traveller and track. With this the helmsman is not only able to correctly position the sail in relation to the wind direction, but to determine its shape. The rule is to flatten the sail for going to windward in strong winds; *a flat sail spills more wind than a full one.* Between the arrows of the larger arc the sail can be adjusted to wind direction. The sail can only be flattened in positions over the smaller arc. Flatten the sail by allowing the traveller to move either side of the centreline (limited by the lanyards) and pull in the mainsheet hard. In light winds the traveller is placed centrally. The mainsheet cannot then be pulled in so hard, therefore the sail

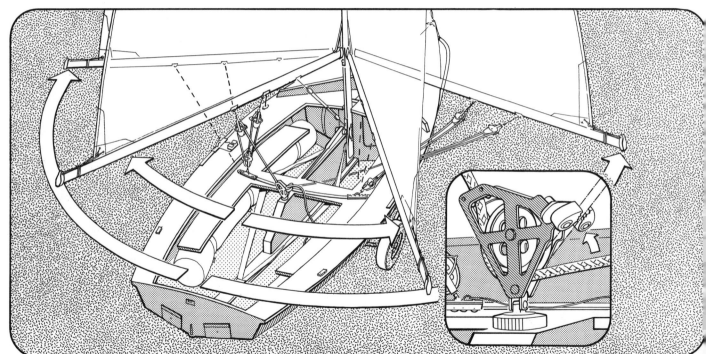

will be fuller, producing maximum effort. The mainsheet shown has a built-in jamb cleat, which helps take the strain off the helmsman's arms. He must be prepared to release quickly to spill excessive wind. Our right-hand illustration shows flexible boom and mast as fitted to many modern dinghies, which aids sail flattening and control.

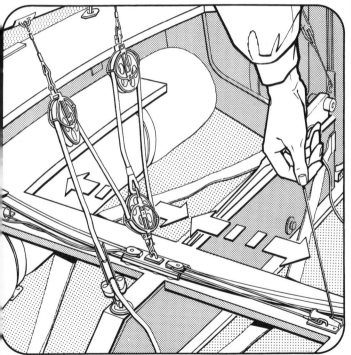

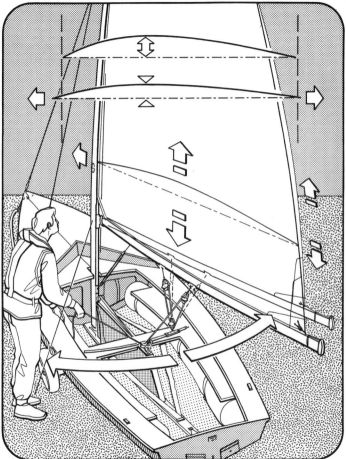

Launching your boat is the final act preparatory to actually sailing. To do this properly and well is an essential part of seamanship and requires some thought, because winds and tides can vary such a lot and so can the places at which you launch.

Basically there are three places from which you will be likely to set off. One is a jetty, the second is a slipway and the third is a beach or similar shore.

Launching from a jetty is clean and easy because your crew can hold the boat at any position while you ship the rudder and check all is in order.

The illustrations show four conditions of wind and tide combined. Boat A, illustrations 1–4, being aware that hoisting sail head to wind not only reduces wear and tear but is much safer also, uses the current or tide to good effect to clear jetty. Boat B's position is next best if the tide is stronger than the wind. Boat C is pinned to the jetty by the tide. Boat A, illustration 3, uses jib only, rounding head to wind before hoisting main.

53

Sailing off a beach on starboard tack with the wind offshore, helmsman climbs aboard while crew holds bow. Ship rudder. Crew then climbs in holding mast to steady himself, pushing boat astern as he does so, while helmsman balances his weight on the other side and prepares to haul in main. Crew aboard, helm is put to port. The crew then pulls in the weather-sheet hard to bring the wind on to the jib in such a way as to push the bow to port.

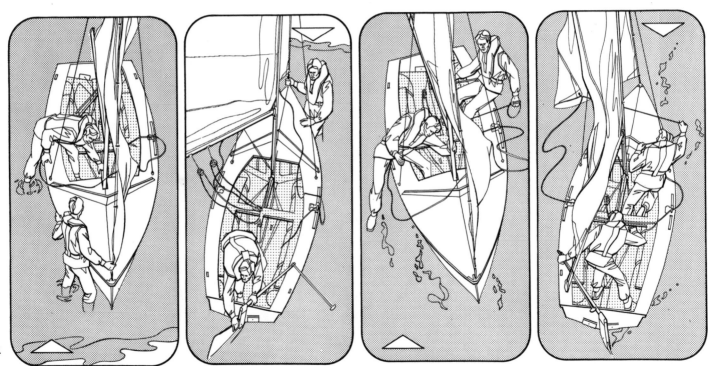

At the same time the boat will move backwards (go astern) and away from the beach. It will soon have turned enough for the mainsheet to be pulled in and the boat sailed off. The jib is, of course, then allowed to set on the leeward side.

The large illustration is a summary of the action. The centre-board is up throughout this manoeuvre.

Launching with the wind along the shore

Mainsail not raised, helmsman steps aboard while crew brings boat round head to wind. Then mainsail is raised single-handed by helmsman (he can take weight off boom on his shoulder).

Ship rudder, crew holding amidships. Rudder blade may not go fully down till boat sails off a little. Note that crew rolls in over side since boat is actually moving in this case – in strong winds it

could gather way fast and crew must waste no time getting aboard. Crew then clambers aboard, while helmsman puts helm up to take boat away from shore. Large drawing shows complete sequence. Note way crew pulls jib to windward to help boat bear away. Remember to put the plate down if you intend a windward course.

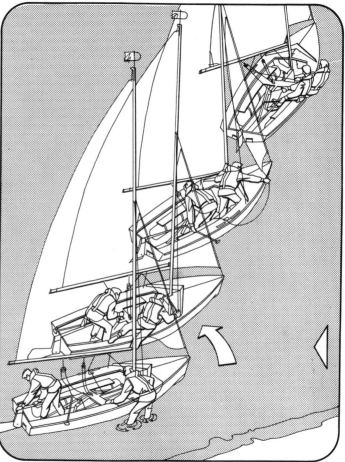

Going off with the wind onshore, it may be necessary to hoist sails when afloat, depending essentially on wind strength and particular area. Crew holds bow and stands deep in the water to facilitate lowering the rudder while the helmsman hoists sail. Crew then moves round to side and rolls in over the deck, pushing bow to port as he does so.

Helmsman puts helm up and bears away. Depending on wind strength, this manoeuvre can be a very fast one and calls for good

 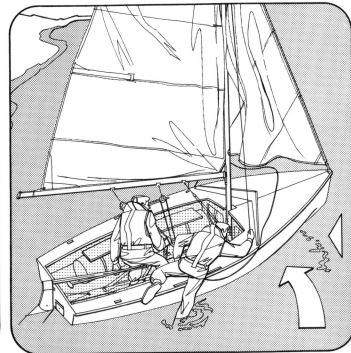

teamwork and speed on part of crew. Remember, you must have enough room to clear shore at approximately 45 degrees from the wind.

Once aboard, the crew lowers the plate as soon as possible and hauls in the jib sheet while the helmsman trims the main for the boat to sail off close-hauled.

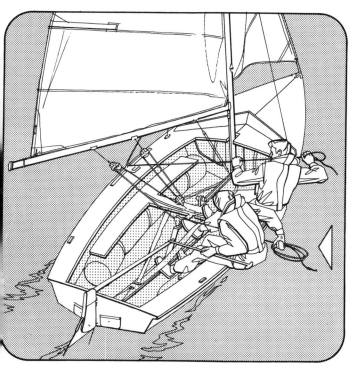

Some useful terms

These terms will help you understand the principles of sailing as explained in this book. It is not a comprehensive list and you will learn other terms as you work through the book, do more sailing and talk to other people. Sailing has its own special language. A command of it is one of the signs of a competent sailor.

Aback- when the wind strikes the wrong side of the sail

Aft-in the back part of the boat

Ahead-in front of the boat

Amidships-in the middle of the boat

Astern-behind the boat

Bear away-to turn the bow away from the wind direction

Beating-sailing close-hauled

Board-distance covered between two tacks

By the lee-when the boat is dead before the wind and the wind starts to get round behind the mainsail. Means you are on the wrong tack and must gybe

Close-hauled-sailing with the sheets as hard in as possible

Course-direction deliberately steered by the helmsman; hence *on course* and *off course*

Down wind-to leeward, away from the wind

Ease sheets-let the sails out

Forward-in the front part of the boat

Free-sailing with the sheets eased

Go about-to tack through the eye of the wind

Gybe-to tack with the wind always from astern

Harden sheets-pull the sails in

Head to wind-bow pointing directly into the wind

Helm down-steering into the wind, tiller away from the wind

Helm up-steering away from the wind, tiller towards the wind

In irons-boat stopped head to wind

Lee shore-with the wind blowing towards the shore or *onshore wind*

Leeward side-side to which the wind is blowing; hence *to leeward*

Leeway-movement sideways due to wind pressure

Luff up-to turn the bow towards the wind direction

Pinching-sailing too close to the wind so that the sails shake

Port-left-hand side of the boat, looking forward

Port tack-sailing with the wind coming over the port side

Reef, to-reduce sail area by rolling it round, or tying it to, the boom with reef points

Starboard-right-hand side of the boat, looking forward

Starboard tack-sailing with the wind coming over the starboard side

To tack-to change sailing direction from one tack to the other; commonly used for 'go about'

Up wind-to windward, towards the wind

Weather shore-with the wind blowing off the shore or *offshore wind*

Windward side-side from which the wind is coming; hence *to windward*

The helmsman must give clear commands to his crew in the correct language e.g. when going about he says 'Ready about' to prepare the crew and 'Lee-o' when he is performing the manoeuvre; similarly 'Stand by to gybe', 'Gybe-o'.

PART 2

Sailing: theory and practice

It helps to know just *why* your boat sails if you want to make it sail properly.

Simply, the wind does not just push your boat along, except immediately before the wind. For the most part the sails act as aerofoils, generating power (called lift), which is then transferred through the spars to the hull. The shape of the boat, the resistance of the water along the hull and against the centreboard, make sure that most of this power is transformed into forward motion, though some of it is lost through the boat going sideways (making *leeway* and *heeling*) and some is lost through the friction of the water and air through which the boat is passing.

No matter what kind of rig your boat has, the principle is the same. Air (wind) flowing over the curved surface of the material of the sail on the windward side causes lift by high pressure. Air flowing over the leeward side also causes lift through low pressure by creating an area of lower pressure. If you have two sails there is an additional effect caused by the air passing between the jib and the mainsail increasing the lift on the leeward side of the mainsail. This is called the slot effect.

Like an aircraft wing, a sail can reach a position of stall. That is, if the wind does not strike it at exactly the right angle, called the *angle of attack*, then the amount of lift will either be nil or lower than it should be. It is, therefore, critical to practise getting the wind to strike the sail just at the right angle – at approximately 22 degrees to apparent wind for maximum aerodynamic force or lift. To ensure that your sails are set at the correct angle, the best thing to do is to ease your sheets until the sails start to shake, then pull them in just far enough for the sail to fill completely. The last portion of the sail to fill will be the *luff* and it is this part which you constantly watch for any sign that your sail trim is incorrect. With enough practice this is something which becomes second nature, anyway. In practice the wind that strikes the sail is not the wind which we should feel on our face if we stood still on land, but an air stream called the apparent wind. We have explained this phenomenon on page 67.

The closest a boat can sail to the true wind is between 42 and 45 degrees. You can, therefore, never sail straight into the wind. A quadrant measuring 45 degrees either side of the true wind is known as the unattainable area. If the destination you want to reach lies in this area you must reach it by a series of tacks *[see page 72]*. You set your sails close to the centreline of the boat *[see page 71]*. Using the rudder you adjust the whole boat to the correct *angle of attack*.

For reaching a destination outside the unattainable quadrant, set the boat in the direction of the destination and adjust the sails as described earlier in this section, so that they are no more than completely filled. All this will become quite clear as you study the drawings on the various points of sailing in the next few pages.

Finally, it is important to realise that the forces generated by the wind are not all converted into driving the boat forward. Some of them are wasted in pushing the boat sideways (heeling and leeway). This loss of power is at its greatest when the boat is close-hauled. Since the forces generated by the wind on the sails are at right angles to the surfaces of the sails, then as the sheets are eased and the sail moves forward and outboard, the direction of the driving force moves nearer to the direction of travel of the boat and loss in sideways movement is less. This is illustrated on page 69.

Finally, we must mention loss of power due to friction of the air and water and the resistance of both these. Keeping the bottom of the boat clean and keeping all above water surfaces as smooth as possible will reduce friction. Resistance of wind and water you can do little about; it mostly depends on the design of your boat. It is just worth remembering that it is at its greatest dead before the wind.

With the sails set at an approximate angle of 22 degrees to the apparent wind (light arrow), viewed from above the camber lines indicate that the sail has taken on its aerofoil shape.

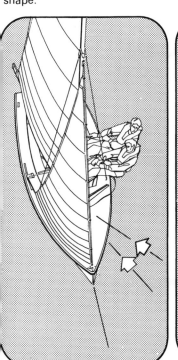

Diagrammatically, jib and main can be viewed as one large aerofoil shape (dotted line). Both are set as close as possible to the boat's centreline.

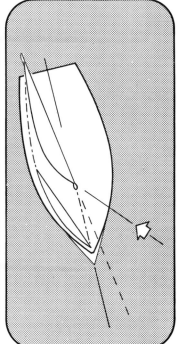

Assuming they work as one aerofoil, air flow (high pressure) on the windward side generates lift.

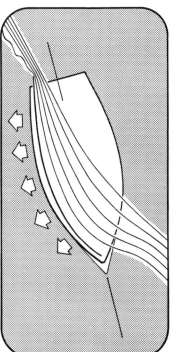

On the leeward side a faster air flow generates an area of low pressure causing even more lift.

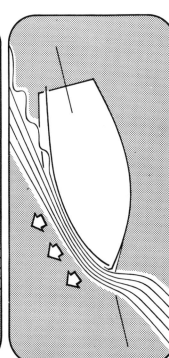

In practice the air flows coincide. Note the turbulence at the rear of the single sail. Where there are in practice two sails, the slot effect, wind funnelling between the jib and the main, will improve lift on the main by increasing air speed over its surface, and reduce turbulence on the main. Here we see the total combined effort of all air flows over the surface of the sails. The best angle between the centreline of the boat and the apparent wind (light arrow) is about 25°. Between the apparent wind and the true wind (dark arrow) there is another 17°. The boat cannot therefore sail closer than 42° to the true wind. A lot of less sophisticated boats cannot get this close as they cannot trim their sails close enough (dotted lines).

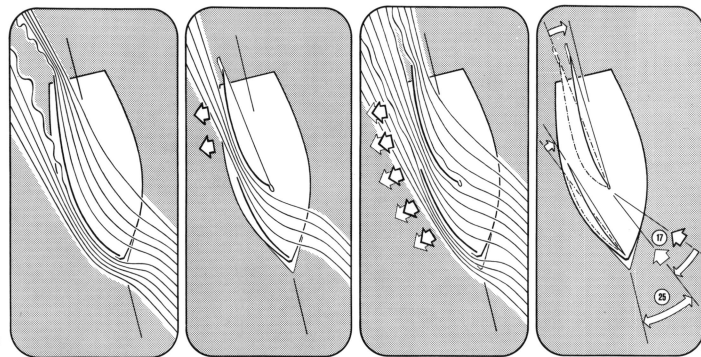

66

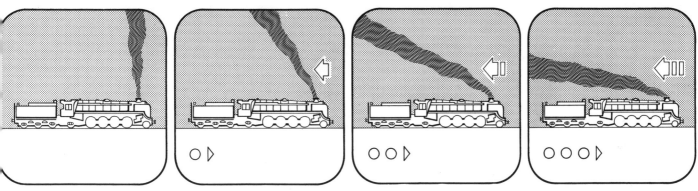

Apparent wind. On a windless day, a train gathers speed. The smoke plume appears to indicate an increasing head wind. This wind is called *own* wind. If there is a *true* wind at right angles to the train (lower diagrams), then as the train gathers speed, *true* wind combines with *own* wind to make *apparent wind* from between *own* and *true* wind. As the train goes faster or slower so the *apparent* wind moves forward or backward. While there is *true* wind at an angle to the train direction, the apparent wind can never come from dead ahead. The same principle applies to wind on sails. It is *apparent* wind that strikes them just as it determines the direction of the train's smoke.

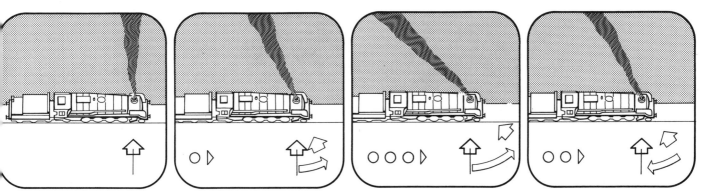

67

Heading into the wind stationary, the boat has no apparent wind, in fact a quadrant measuring 42° either side of the true wind's direction is unobtainable.

As the boat bears away and picks up speed so the apparent wind starts to move ahead until the boat reaches its maximum close-hauled speed. The apparent wind is now approximately 17° ahead of the true wind. To go faster would mean bearing away further and using the aerodynamic forces more efficiently.

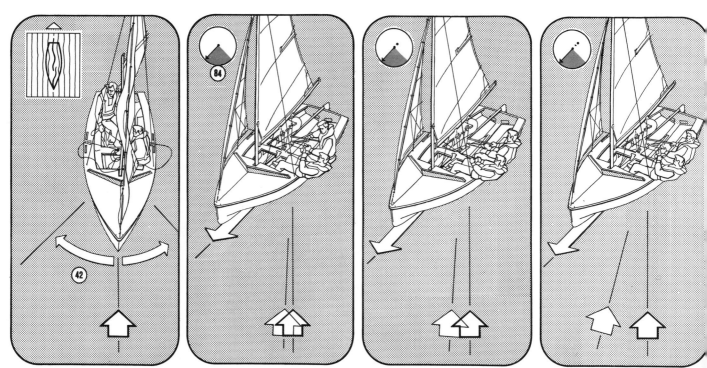

The aerodynamic force acts at 90° to the sails (white arrow). This force is resisted by the centreboard and hull shape, although some movement sideways (leeway) occurs. In resisting leeway, the boat is forced to heel (dark arrow); this is countered by sitting further outboard. Finally movement forward is made. Heeling movement and leeway (combined in dark arrow) diminish as the sails are re-set to a close reach. An increase in speed occurs due to more favourable use of the driving force. An even more favourable force direction produces very little leeway, due to increased speed. Crew can reduce the board area. With the wind aft, lift is not possible, only air pressure. Sail positions now make the maximum use of this; speed is drastically reduced due to lower power and greater resistance.

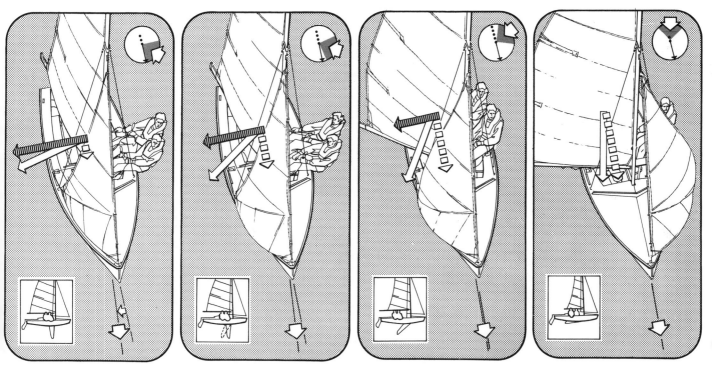

69

If we set our crew the task of sailing a large circle and observe them from upwind, they will sail through all the points of sailing possible. Should they hold course anywhere on the circle they can in fact sail in any direction except 42 degrees (plus leeway approx 45 degrees) either side of the true wind, indicated by the shaded area, small circle wind clock.

Sailing down wind (running). Mainsail working by wind pressure only is blanketing the jib Mainsheet freed! Helmsman sheets in (right), puts the helm down a little on to a broad reach, air flow over the main sail improves, jib – now opening to the wind – fills, and some aerodynamic force is generated, speed increases, apparent winds starts to move forward.

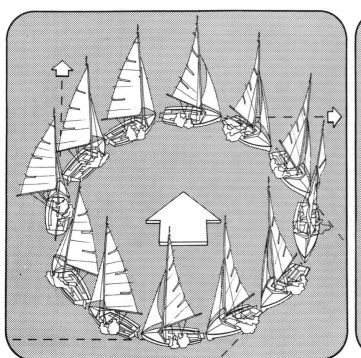

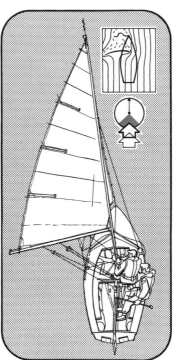

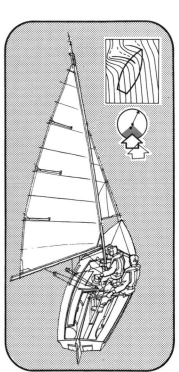

The boat is now on a broad reach (left). Aerodynamic force greatly improved, helmsman and crew adjusting sails to the new apparent wind which continues to move forward. They now need to sit further out to counteract heeling force, speed still increasing which will minimise leeway.

The boat is now sailing (reaching) (inner left) a very fast course on which planing could occur [see page 86].

Reaching (inner right). Across the wind, the speed is still considerable.

The boat, now going to windward (right), begins to experience maximum leeway and heel, and as a result speed will drop.

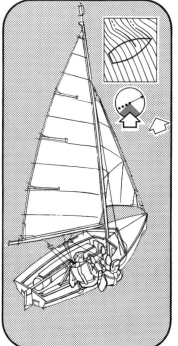
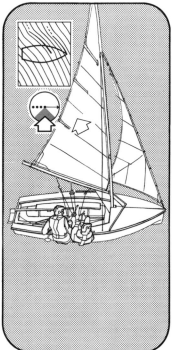

Across these two pages we show the sequence of tacking, going through the eye of the wind from the starboard tack to the port tack. The small diagrams indicate the wind flow over the sails and the shaded sections in the small circles indicate the area of the wind clock in which the boat cannot sail. You must have sufficient speed on the boat to carry its head through the area in which no driving force is generated.

In the third picture you will note that the crew is holding the jib so that the wind will blow the head of the boat round. This is only necessary if your boat tacks slowly, or you have misjudged the

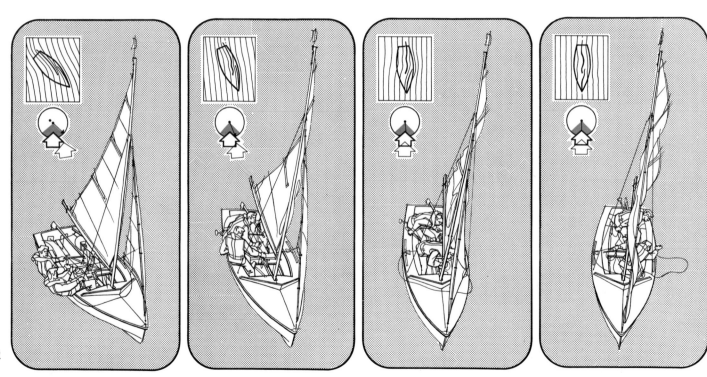

speed needed or the wind is very light. Normally the crew can just let the jib go completely as soon as the helmsman puts the helm down and says 'Lee-o'. Preparatory to tacking he should always warn his crew by saying 'Ready to tack'.

Seven pictures show the sequence of the tack in detail while the eighth shows how by a series of tacks the boat makes its way into the wind. It cannot sail straight into the wind, but it can zigzag its way there. Note: for this manoeuvre you always need the centreboard fully down.

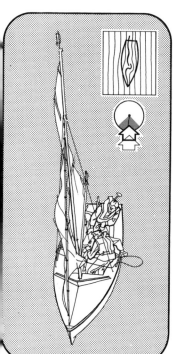

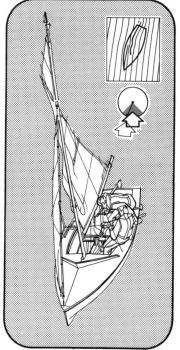

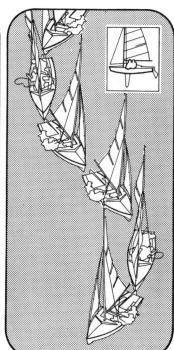

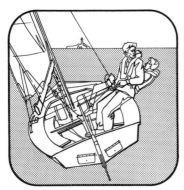   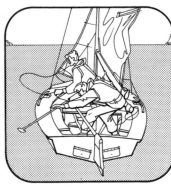

Here we see the precise actions of the helmsman in the act of tacking viewed from astern. Note how he looks round first to see that all is clear for him to tack, then he bears away slightly to get maximum speed for the manoeuvre.

You will also see that at the exact moment of coming head to wind when he is changing sides, he lets the tiller go having previously made sure that the extension (if any) has been pushed over ready for him to pick up quickly. He changes hands on mainsheet and tiller.

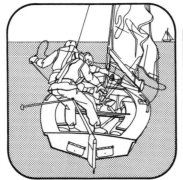 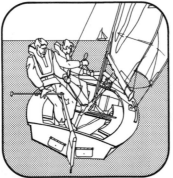 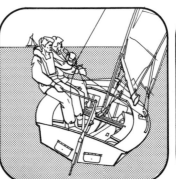 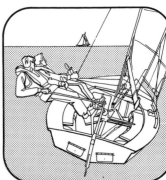

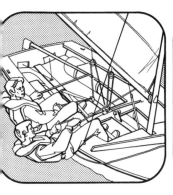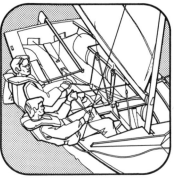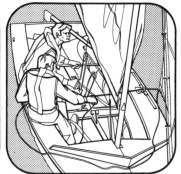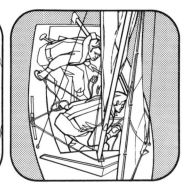

The crew viewed from forward in the same circumstances. Helmsman is warning him of his intention to tack with the command 'Ready about'. Crew frees the jib sheet, on the order 'Lee-o', he removes feet from toe straps and shifts his weight across the centre line, timing his move to coincide with the boom's swing. *Important:* crew must remember to pull plenty of slack through fairlead as he lets fore sheet go or it may foul as he hauls in on new tack. Smooth, precise actions by both crew are important to achieve competent tacking.

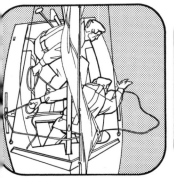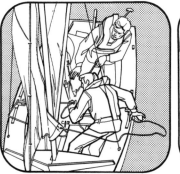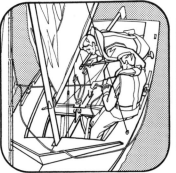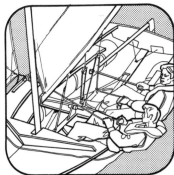

Here we have the sequence of bearing away from the close-hauled position to broad reaching. The small diagrams show roughly how much centreboard you need on each point of sailing to give you good control and trim. You will notice that the crew does not need to sit out so far as the boat attains the reaching position, since less of the wind force is expended on heeling the boat.

The helmsman should endeavour to put his helm up and ease his sheets as one smooth action when bearing away.

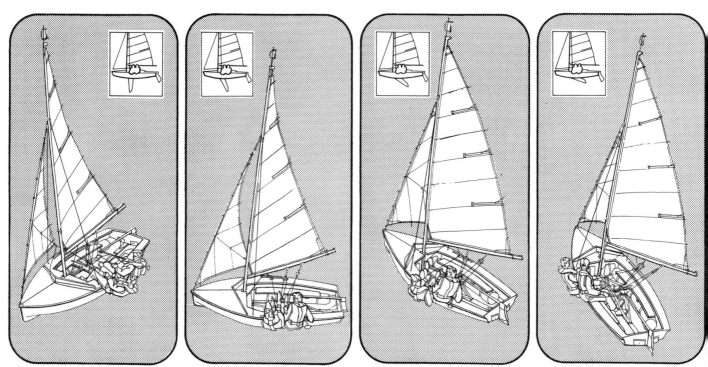

The crew are now coming to the last position of all, running dead before the wind. To complete a full circle you can either pull your sheets in again and come up towards the wind until you have to tack or you can gybe.

Before explaining this manoeuvre we show the running position in detail, with the centreboard right up and the jib pulled out on the windward side to keep it filled. This is called *goose-winging* the sail.

When running, you must always watch the wind constantly to see that it does not get behind the mainsail (by the lee) and so cause an accidental gybe.

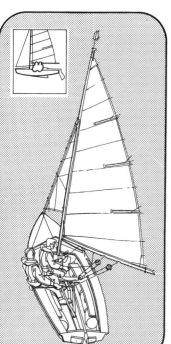

Gybing safely in strong winds means correct balance and good co-ordination of movements.

Firstly steer the boat so that she is dead before the wind and perfectly upright. Keep the centreboard up to reduce sideways resistance. Then steer to bring the wind from just behind the mainsail. Crew moves to centre and grasps boom to help it across under control. Helmsman keeps the boat on course – this is very important because if he loses control the boat can screw round and capsize. When the boom is centred or across, return course to dead before the wind and goose-wing the jib.

Small circles show clearly wind and boat directions at stages of gybing.

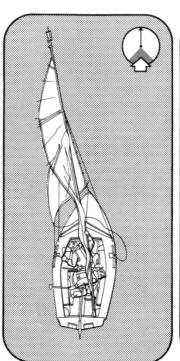
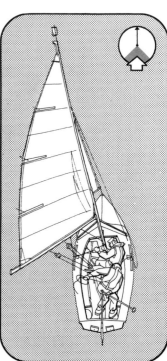

The first picture shows a very bad gybe, known as a Chinese gybe. Caused by a slack kicking strap *[see page 49]*, a very free mainsheet and the crew failing to pass the boom across. You risk a torn sail or a capsize. Cure is to gybe back immediately and start again.

To run steadily, goose-wing the jib. In light airs the helmsman can hold jib sheet to leeward while crew hold main boom. A whisker pole as illustrated is perfect. The crew is then able to control both main boom and jib leaving helmsman to steer and work out tactics.

Running before the wind, especially without a whisker pole, there is a danger of the boat rolling badly in strong winds. If the jib pulls *all* the time it helps damp down rolling. The situation can become serious if you allow the mainsail to go too far forward as illustrated. The boat starts to screw in an uncontrollable way until it rolls over to windward, one of the commonest reasons for a capsize. To prevent this, keep the main from going forward of mast and keep jib pulling to balance boat.

Here is a capsize due to rolling downwind. Take care jumping past the boat and its gear. Never leave the boat to retrieve any gear which may be floating away. All loose gear should be secured anyway before you start. The crew in the water, acting as a sea anchor, can turn the boat head to wind by holding bow, and helmsman stops boat going right over until she is head to wind.

If the wind is very fresh or the crew after one or two attempts cannot right the boat, crew moves aft to lower sail before they try again. If the boat turns turtle (turns right over) then exert pull, as indicated bottom left.

When boat is righted, secure sail while crew holds boat head to wind.

All light dinghies without fixed keels can capsize and the risk is always there in fresh to strong winds. Do everything you can to avoid a capsize. It can be dangerous; at very least it is uncomfortable and you may need to be rescued because you cannot guarantee to right a capsized boat under all conditions of wind and tide.

Capsizing occurs usually through bad seamanship. We have just dealt with the effects of rolling downwind. You can stop rolling downwind altogether if you sail downwind in a series of reaches, instead of running. The boat will sail faster and much more steadily.

If you do not control a gybe, then you may broach to and capsize. If the wind is so strong and the sea so rough that you fear this may happen, then tack instead of gybing, but be sure you come up into the wind gently.

Broaching-to means suddenly coming up into the wind where you have been sailing on a broad reach or run. The reason a boat capsizes when broached to is that the wind pressure is all used to heel the boat over instead of drive it forward.

A common cause of capsize for beginners is failure to release the mainsheet fast enough when sailing close-hauled and the boat is hit by a sudden squall. Never cleat the mainsheet until you have mastered the ability to release it instantly if there is too much wind pressure on the sail for safety.

In strong winds, then, it is important to keep your boat moving. Never allow her to stop and then suddenly, with the sails sheeted hard in, be hit by a gust of wind. This will drive the boat over sideways rather than forward.

In a capsize stay with the boat, never swim after gear or try to reach another boat or the shore.

Don't struggle to right a boat if you are becoming exhausted. Save your energies and wait for help. An exhausted man can suffer very quickly from exposure.

You should know how to right your own particular boat. If you want to practise, do it on a calm day, close to the shore where you can stand if necessary, but you will need sufficient depth of water for the boat to come up with the board right down!

Quickly bail enough water out for the crew to come aboard. Get him in over the stern, use a stirrup if necessary (tie a loop in the mainsheet with a bowline and make the end fast to the main thwart). While there is still water in the boat it will be risky to try to pull him in over the side. This could cause another capsize.

Self-bailers or stern flaps as illustrated are a great help in ridding the boat of water once it can be got on the move. They are worth fitting to any light dinghy because they get rid of spray in rough weather too.

If you lose a man overboard you can either heave to (back jib head to wind) so he can swim to you, or return immediately to pick him up. Weather, sea and tide will dictate the method adopted. The important thing is to correctly judge your return in the conditions. Left. With the wind aft, Boat A turns immediately and so retains a windward approach. Inner left. Sailing into or across the wind Boat A again retains windward manoeuvrability, but this time by delaying his turn. B in both cases is downwind. Inner right. This course avoids the gybe which could be dangerous with only one man on board in rough weather. Right. It is better to come up just to windward and drift down giving the man in the water some protection by the boat's lee. It also gives you

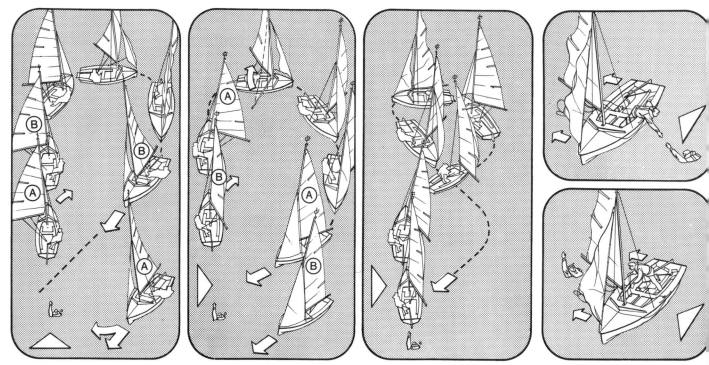

time to free the sheet, fully off, and get a line ready. This manoeuvre is only safe in a light dinghy.

With the sails up it will be virtually impossible to get your man on board without capsizing. If he is unable to help himself, make him fast alongside, looping a bowline under his arms. Then take down the mainsail, head to wind, and remove the rudder. Manoeuvre your man aft and haul him in over the transom. The average dinghy is not stable enough to haul someone over the side, though they might be able to clamber in if you put your weight on the opposite gunwale. The stern has the greatest stability fore and aft. If the man has been in the water some time and is exhausted, signal for assistance [see page 95].

The fastest point of sailing for a dinghy is planing, but to be able to do this a boat must have flat sections aft and a long, straight keel. It can then develop the lift under the hull from the water which will enable it to skim along at speeds twice or three times as great as normal. You also need at least a wind speed of 10–12 knots. A planing dinghy leaves its normal stern wave far behind, while its bow wave moves aft as the hull lifts. If the boat buries its nose while planing, immediately free the jib.

In the large illustration you see a dinghy in the planing attitude and accelerating.

As the planing dinghy accelerates, so will the apparent wind move ahead and the sails have to be trimmed in to allow for this or the sails will not develop their maximum power. A planing dinghy, then, will always appear to be nearly close-hauled even if it is sailing a long way off the true wind.

The first illustration shows the helmsman aware of the approaching wind force which will accelerate the dinghy on to a true planing position.

The same effect as trimming the sheets can be obtained by bearing away slightly as the boat accelerates, though you will still eventually have to trim the sheets a bit.

This is the most exciting and exhilarating point of sailing.

The spinnaker is a useful extra sail before the wind. You need a special halyard for the spinnaker, running above the forestay with a quick release swivel clip as illustrated. Before hoisting, lead the sheet and guy aft, making sure that they go *outside* the forestay. The helmsman holds them or belays them temporarily until the crew has the pole in position.

Hoist with one hand letting the spinnaker run through the other so it cannot fill too soon. Attach pole as indicated first to tack of sail and then to mast. Note quick release fittings on either end of boom. A topping lift on the pole will ensure good control *[see detail page 90]*. Inset bottom right-hand illustration this page, for suggested method of fitting.

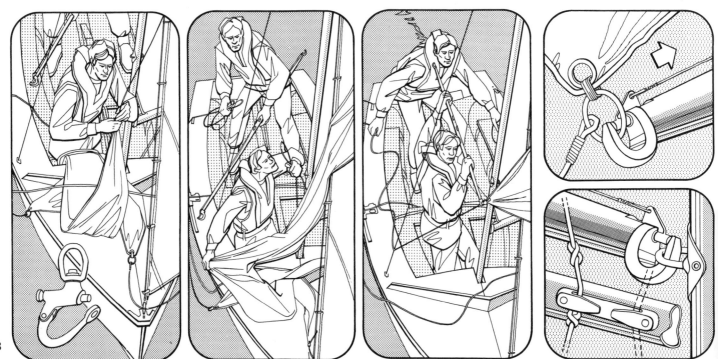

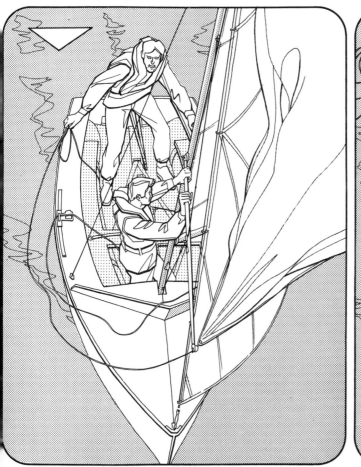

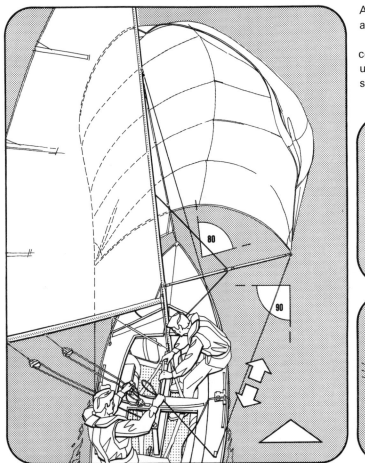

After adjusting the spinnaker pole approximately 80° to the mast and 90° to the wind's direction, you are ready to trim the spinnaker.

Small illustrations show: Spinnaker backwinding main, corrected by easing sheet. Broad reach with spinnaker, crew take up position to counter heel. The limit to which you can use spinnaker with wind forward of beam.

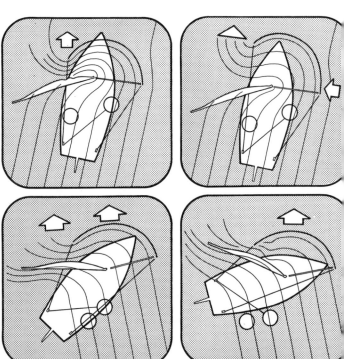

In this sequence of gybing under spinnaker you take the mainsail over first. Then simply reverse the ends of the spinnaker pole. Your spinnaker pole topping lift should be made of shock cord to facilitate this. The helmsman steers with his legs playing the sheet and guy as necessary. If the action is done smoothly, the spinnaker can be kept filled as you perform the change-over.

To lower the spinnaker, remove pole from mast, draw in tack of sail and release from pole. Ease guy off. Draw sail in quickly *under* the boom.

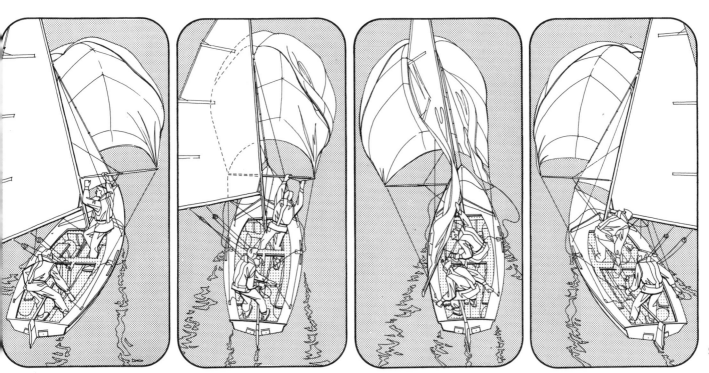

Starboard tack rule – the most fundamental rule of the road. Left. When two boats are sailing close-hauled the boat on the starboard tack (wind coming over starboard side) has right of way. Illustrations 1–4 show the port tack boat tacking to avoid collision. He could have gone astern of the starboard tack boat and held his general course. But remember the increase in speed when bearing away. By tacking, both boats – if a collision occurs – will be travelling in the same basic direction and damage will be minimised. Dinghies are in danger of collision when three boat lengths apart and on converging courses.

To avoid collision, when two sailing boats approach one another, remember: When each has the wind on a different side, the vessel

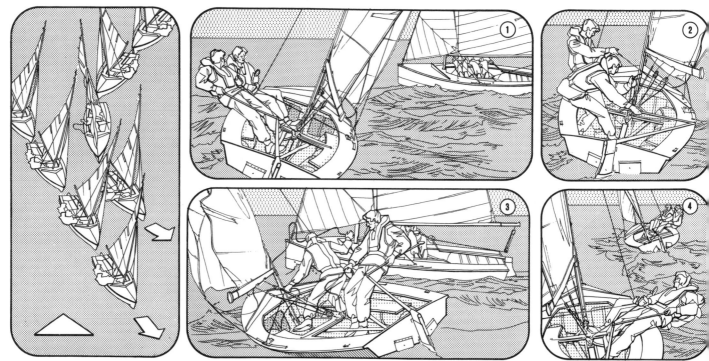

which has port side wind shall avoid the other; when each has the wind on the same side, the vessel which is to windward shall avoid the leeward vessel. Every vessel overtaking any other shall keep clear of the vessel overtaken; the boat with right of way still has an obligation to avoid collision if the boat without right of way doesn't respond. In the illustration, the starboard tack boat is giving way because the port tack boat has held her course. Your duty is to avoid crossing *ahead* of another boat. Take early action to avoid risk of collision. When in doubt, go astern of the boat with the right of way.

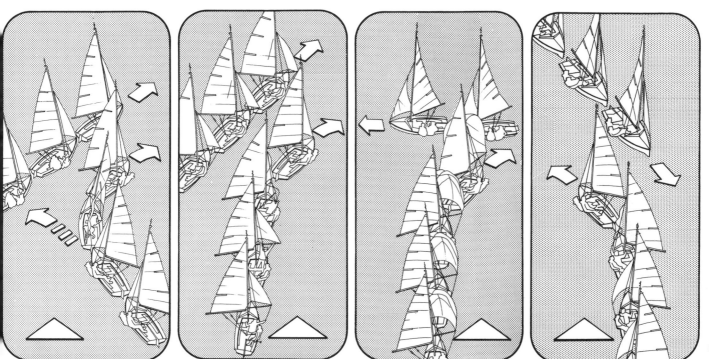

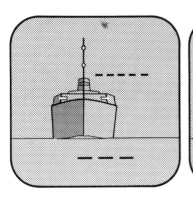 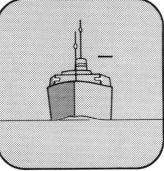  

Normally, power gives way to sail, but in all restricted waters seagoing vessels have absolute right of way over pleasure craft.

Five short blasts: 'Get out of my way', three long blasts: 'I am going astern'; one long blast: 'I am turning to starboard'. Check this is happening. The masts will separate as she turns. Two long blasts: 'I am turning to port'.

It is dangerous to cross the bows of a large ship; vessels pass, in opposite directions, port to port. Watch for course alterations. When power vessels are converging, the vessel with the other on the starboard side gives way. *At all times* keep well away from shipping. Think before enforcing right of way. In the drawing the cruiser would run aground if she had to tack. She might be under power as well.

 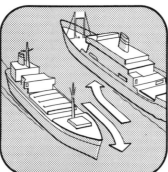  

While we assume that you will always try to sail safely, it is as well to know the accepted signals for distress. You may be able to help a fellow seaman in trouble. The illustrations are quite self-explanatory, showing recognised distress signals both sound and visual. If you intend to cruise, even in a dinghy, we recommend that you equip your boat with red signal flares and smoke flares, the latter for use at night and the former during the day.

A few tips for better sailing: Constantly check wind direction and speed.

Watch for squalls with offshore winds.

Sea breezes are generally steady.

Tides are strongest 2 to 3 hours either side of high water.

Wind and current together: smooth sea.

Wind against current: choppy sea.

Approaching objective shorten tacks to save sailing too far. Dotted line shows new course if wind shifts.

In light winds, constantly watch for puffs. Adjust heading of boat. Crew well forward. Easing to windward.

In choppy water, sail freer and faster. Crew slightly aft. Go too close and the waves stop you.

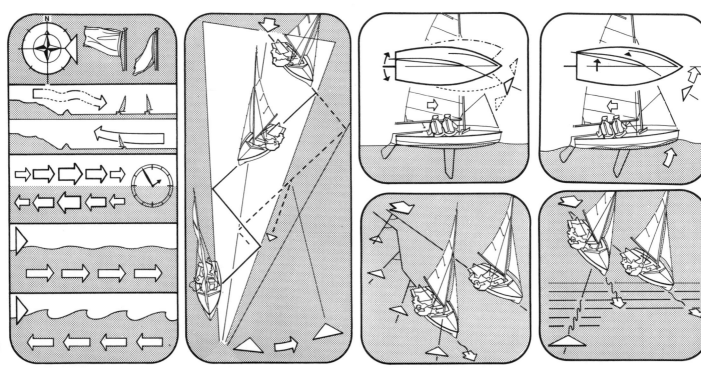

Head up above the course you want to follow to compensate for leeway. Currents can increase effects of leeway.

Use the current or allow for it when you choose your course.

When current is against you, make short tacks across it, and long tacks with it.

When current is with you, tacks across it pay off.

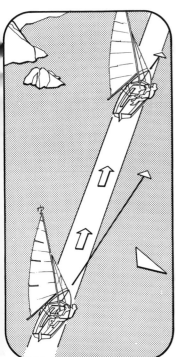

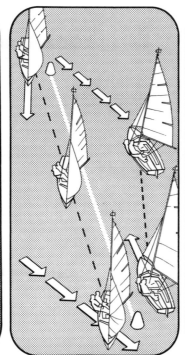

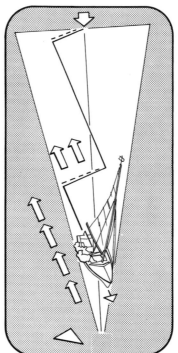

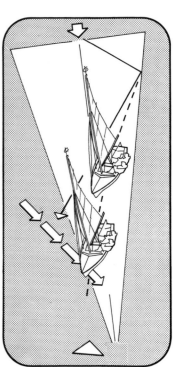

Sailing to pick up a mooring or finding an anchoring position can be similar to picking up a man overboard. Wind against the tide, use a jib only. Have a line already made fast on the boat and pass it through the eye of mooring buoy.

Leaving or picking up a mooring, wind and tide together or where there is no current use full sail and cast off on the windward side. Leaving a mooring wind against tide, use jib only, cast off on windward side. When in clear water, round up head to wind and hoist main.

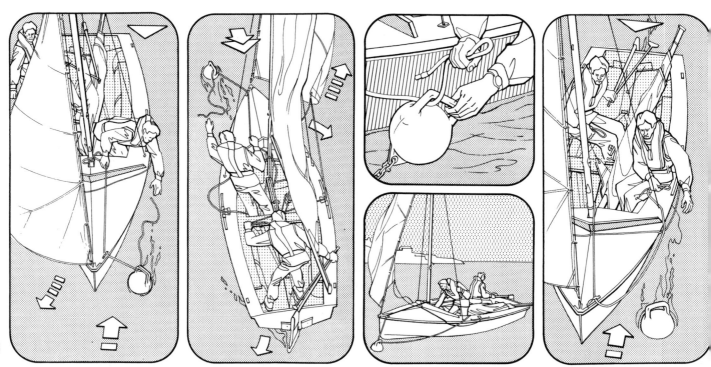

Never sail without an anchor and warp. It may be your only means of preventing yourself drifting out to sea with the tide. To anchor safely you need six times as much warp as the depth of water before the anchor bites. Check against a shore mark to see if your anchor is holding. Do not lower sail until sure. If wind is against tide, a bucket trailed astern, centreboard and rudder down will stop swinging. Wind and tide together reduce drag. Centreboard and rudder up. Break out anchor, by hauling up or sailing over to break out. For a dinghy, a small folding anchor is ideal. Less damage likely to air bags. For neatness, store warp on a drum. Amount of warp carried will depend on depth of water in which you are likely to anchor. 10–15 fathoms is a useful length.

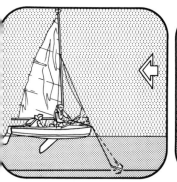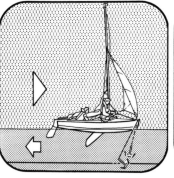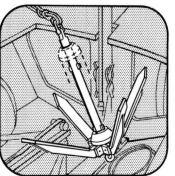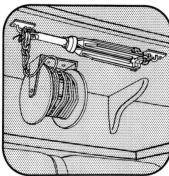

Coming ashore on a beach in an onshore wind – come in with jib only, centreboard up, rudder up, or off if fixed, use paddle for steerage but watch out for heavy swell. Get the boat clear of the water quickly.

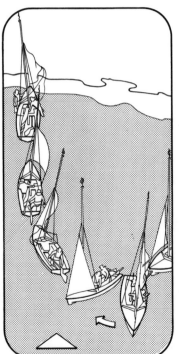

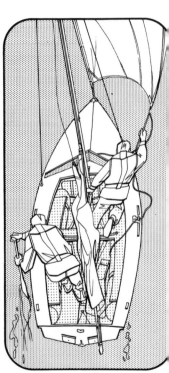

Left. Coming ashore with wind offshore. Centre. With wind along the shore. Don't forget to take into account the depth of the water and any tides. Don't step overboard until you are sure you can stand no more than waist deep.

Right. Coming alongside a jetty or slipway. If you have a choice always come up to the leeward side, but in any case do your manoeuvres gently. To do it well means getting to know exactly how to control your speed as though you had an engine. It just takes practice. Note boat A has performed a good manoeuvre.

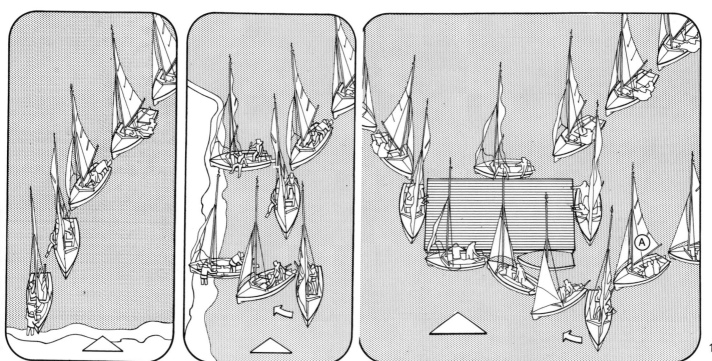

PART 3

Knots, splices and whippings

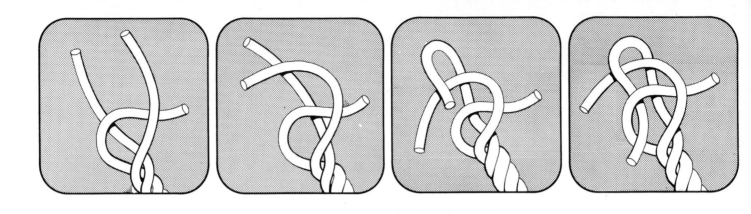

A back splice – method of neatly finishing off the end of a rope, though not where it has to pass through a block frequently. Ideal for keeping the crew on their toes!

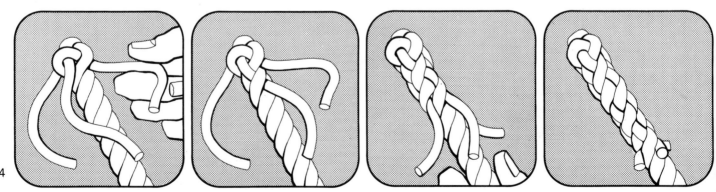

An eye splice – a most useful splice which can be done with or without a thimble in the middle. Finish off neatly with seizing as illustrated.

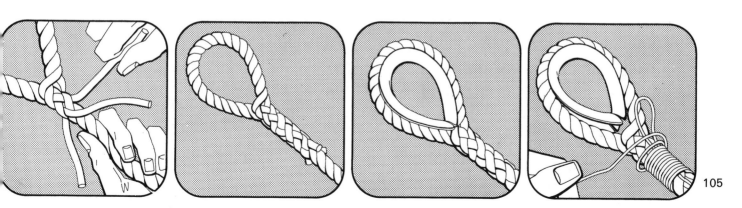

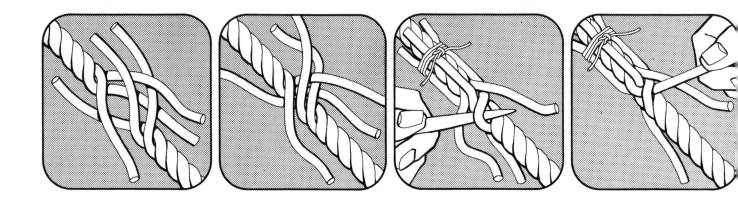

A short splice – for joining two pieces of equal size rope together. Not particularly neat, but strong. You need at least three tucks each side for safety.

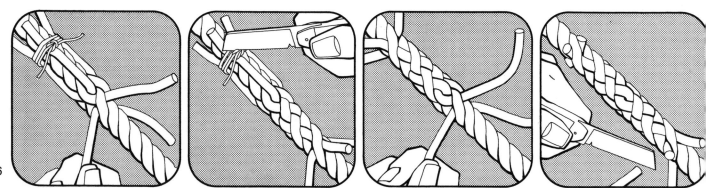

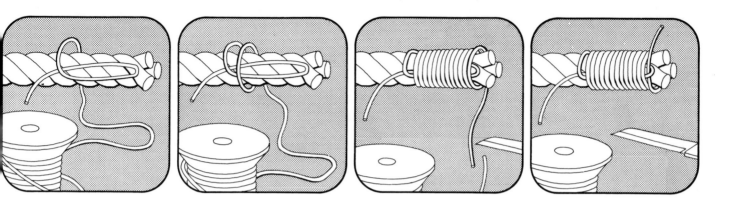

Plain whipping – a very neat way of finishing off the end of a sheet or halyard. Even if you heat-seal synthetic rope it is better and more seamanlike to finish off with a whipping. Last two drawings in sequence show an alternative method of whipping.

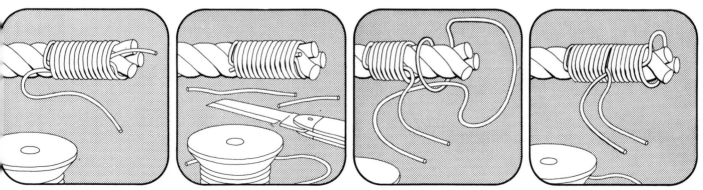

107

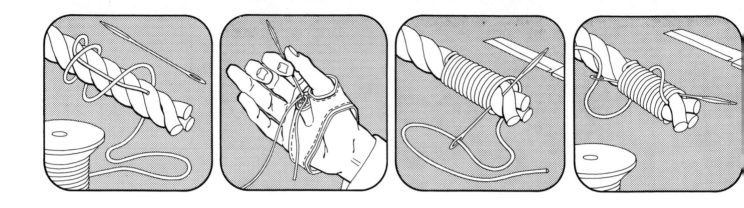

Palm and needle whipping – more difficult to do, but it makes a much stronger and lasting finish to a rope's end. The true mark of a seaman!

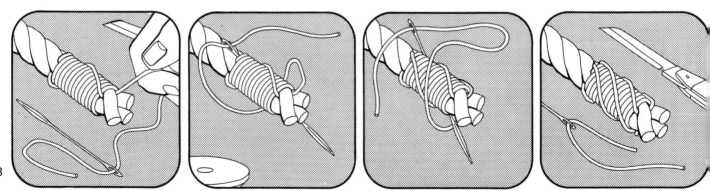

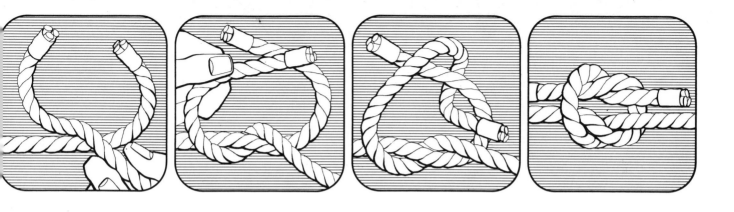

A reef knot. With ropes of equal thickness it cannot slip. The bottom line of drawings shows one method of getting it undone if it is very tight. Bottom, extreme right; method of tying a reef knot with quick release.

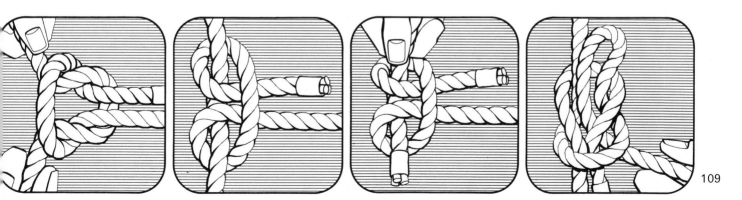

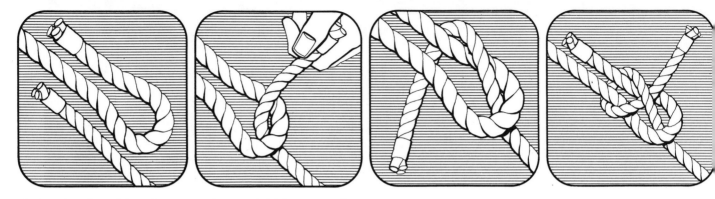

A sheet bend used for tying ropes of unequal thickness together.

This can be tied with a quick release (extreme left). Remaining three illustrations show a double sheet bend, which is much more secure than the single.

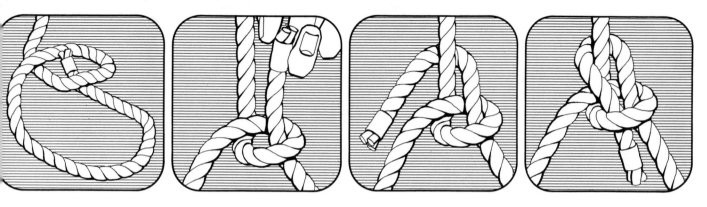

A bowline – this knot just cannot slip if tied properly, so ideal for tying round people!

A round turn and two half hitches – an easy safe way to tie a dinghy to a ring or bar.

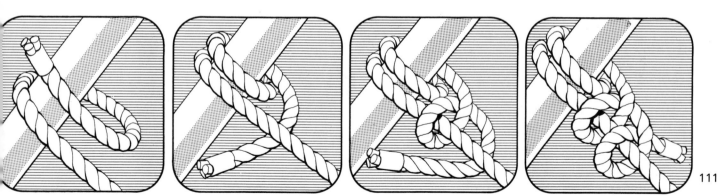

A clove hitch – the ideal knot for making fast to a mooring post.

An anchor bend – an ideal knot for making your warp fast to the anchor. For safety seize tail to standing part, especially if you us
synthetic ropes.

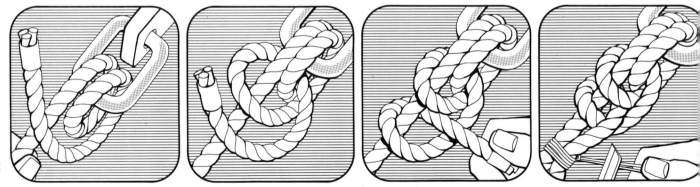